CW01512052

SAY YES

The Hidden Laws of Business
Performance from World-Class Sport

By

Sheena L.C. Walker

Say Yes

A CIP catalogue record for this title is available from the British Library.

Dedication

To my beloved Mum,

Your strength, kindness, and belief have shaped the very foundation of who I am.

To my wonderful children, Gavin, Neil, Fraser, and Isla, your steadfast support and love have been the heartbeat of my journey. You have encouraged, uplifted, and reminded me to dream bigger.

To the sports coaches who first set me on the path to podium performance, thank you for instilling in me the discipline, determination, and desire to excel.

To my lecturers at the University of Stirling, your academic brilliance and belief in possibilities have helped me discover my voice and vision.

And to the world-class thought leaders who have ignited my learning and inspired my legacy,

Tony Robbins, Andy Harrington, Brendon Burchard, Robin Sharma, and many others, you have helped shape the excellence I now teach.

This book is a tribute to all of you for walking with me, believing in me, and helping me design a life of performance, purpose, and podium success.

With deepest gratitude,

Sheena

Preface

A simple question – that sparked a conversation - then a lasting friendship.

I first met Sheena when she came to the BBC to present one of her dynamic, invigorating sessions.

She helped staff become more confident and disciplined to deliver success, both at work and in life more generally.

I was intrigued and wanted to find out more, so I took the initiative to go for a chat.

I can't even remember what I asked her now, but her impact continues to influence me and countless others who've benefitted from her wisdom and continuous learning.

Sheena's so inspiring and encouraging - a passionate advocate for development and improvement.

Her expertise makes her laser-focused, and her superlative methods help people maximise their potential.

Her sunny nature, great humour and endless curiosity about finding new ways to excel make her a real pleasure to be mentored by.

She won't sugarcoat it. She can be tough – even brutal - about where you're going wrong and where you need help, but she has the tools and guidance to help you get there.

And she'll make you laugh. She has a real gift.

But you have to do your homework and play your part; if you don't engage, practice and perfect, then you're wasting an invaluable opportunity for growth.

I feel privileged and honoured to be her friend and be mentored by her.

Since meeting she's selflessly given her time, support and belief in me, to help me become the best version of myself.

This book distils all her hard work, commitment and stimulating guidance to rouse you to act.

You can't help but feel motivated to try harder and be better.

It's a recipe for a successful, stimulating life.

Miss it and you'll miss out.

"Sheena's a dynamic shot of sunshine who energises you to excel." Trudi Barber, BBC Language Services TV Unit
New Broadcasting House

Table of Contents

Dedication iii

Preface iv

Prologue 13

Different Stages 17

The Art of Infinite Coaching 18

The Laser Leadership Archetypes 20

The Training Edge Creator 21

Crafting Enchanting Customer Experiences..............22

The Master Mentor Formula......................................23

The Prosperity of Wealth and Wellbeing 24

Chapter 1 The Podium Performance Booster...............27

Great Ones Plan with Class 27

What Successful People Do Differently 28

From Disruption to Planning with Class 28

Green Light of Obsession 29

Be the Greatest Showman..31

A Giant Life Starts with Giant-Class Thinking 32

Does Your Class Allow You to Go the Extra Mile?..34

Could You Plan Your Winning Performance the Ferrari
Way? 35

How Can You Win Beyond the Arena? 36

Nothing Changes Until Your Mission Becomes Your
Obsession...37

When You Hit a Boulder, Bounce Back 39

Is Your Work a Craft or Class Act? 40

Could You Lead the Field in a New Market? 41

Inspire Others Through a Winning Environment 42

Three DNA Strategies of Champions Determined to Win 44

Winning with High-Performance Goals 46

Raise Your Ambitions 48

Peak Performance Pyramid 49

Scorecard of Critical Success 50

Fast-Forward Feedback 52

Chapter 2 Different Stages of Speaking 55

Is Speaking a Natural Talent? 57

Commanding the Room: From Page to Stage 59

My Future in the World of Performance 60

Mic Drop Moments That Drive Business Results 63

Stellar Speaking Skills in the Corporate World 63

Global Mark Keynote Speaker 67

Becoming an Influential Event Speaker 67

Avoiding Common Pitfalls 68

Ten Characteristics of Performance Speakers 68

Speech Structuring in Various Contexts 70

The Boardroom Backwards Melody 71

The Art and Craft of Stage Presence 74

The Power of Vocal Dynamics 77

Crafting Memorable Stories 78

Principles of a Great Presentation........................... 79

The Power of Scenes 79

TED-Style Speaking (Technical, Entertaining, Design) 80

Chapter 3 The Art of Infinite Coaching 84

World-Class Athletes Have World-Class Coaches.... 86

Coaching for Performance 87

A Great Coach Will Teach and Motivate!................ 87

Authors Specialising as Editors........................... 88

Coaching in Political Campaigns 88

Where Speakers Become World-Class Communicators 89

Are You the Masterpiece or a Self-Proclaimed Expert? 90

Time to Pause, Reset, and Re-engineer Your System 91

Chapter 4 Laser Leadership Archetypes 98

Dare to Embrace a Different Approach 100

Law One: The Winning Difference of a Scientific Laser Leader.. 100

Law Two: Who is to Blame? Who Makes Decisions?... 102

Law Three: Dynamics of Design Thinking 105

Law Four: The Design Thinking Leader 106

Law Five: To Lead a Giant Life Starts with Giant-Class Thinking 109

Law Six: Do Ambassadorial Leaders Achieve Extraordinary Performance? 110

Law Seven: Do Leaders Risk More Than Is Required? 111

Law Eight: Military Leadership The Burden of Command 112

Law Nine: The Methodical Leader in The Boardroom 114

Chapter 5 The Training Edge Creator 118

Law One: Self-Master the Art of Training 121

Law Two: What is Thinking in Design Training? ... 122

Law Three: Adopt Training Design Skills 123

Law Four: Training Versus Teaching 124

Law Five: Design Trainers Are Influential Specialists 125

Law Six: Does Your Class Allow You to Go the Extra Mile? 126

Law Seven: Are You Risking More Than Necessary in Training? 128

Law Eight: When Performance Arrives, Preparation Has Gone 130

Law Nine: Be a Genius and Showcase Your Mastery in Your Performance 133

Law Ten: Create an Outstanding Training Session How? 135

Chapter 6 Crafting Enchanting Customer Experiences 139

Habit One: Securing Customer Approval is the Path Forward.. 140

Habit Two: Build Your Reputation, Become Notable in Your Industry 142

Habit Three: Embracing Our Inner Superstar Qualities.. 144

Habit Four: How Can You Cultivate a Unique Market Niche?.. 145

Habit Five: Celebrities Dream Big and Start Small 147

Habit Six: Develop a Distinctive Personality and Core Values 148

Habit 7: Excel as an Oscar Winner in the Marketplace 150

Habit 8: Why Customers Don't Choose You, Is This Serious? 152

Habit 9: Three Magic Words for Handling Complaints.. 153

Chapter 7 The Master Mentor Machine 157

How Can You Be That Great Advancement? 157

The Body of a Ferrari with a Bicycle Mind............ 159

Greatness Starts Outside Your Comfort Zone......... 160

The Simplicity of Mentoring Sophistication 161

Every New Mentor Wants to Discover the Essential Questions 162

The Luxury Brand Formula 163

Genius Questions for Luxury Brands 163

Celebrity Mentoring Renowned Brands 165

Questions that Spark Performance Discussions 166

Mastermind Mentoring 167

Three Key Influences for Producers 168

One: Mastermind groups 168

Mentors Who Take Centre Stage in the
Boardroom 169

Chapter 8 The Prosperity of Wealth and Wellbeing.... 173

Your A1 Lane: Crafting a New Routine 175

The Five Intentions for A1 Vitality in a Perfect
Morning 178

Do or Ditch Brain Clutter 183

Quality Recovery Builds Resilience Creating White
Space 183

Sheena's Mind, Brain Speaker Shed 184

Busting the Myths of Resilience 185

Resilience: How You Recharge, Not How You
Persevere 186

Is Elon Musk Working in Economy or First Class? 187

Does Streamlining Sleep Create Physical and
Psychological Preparedness? 189

Well-being and Women in Power, or Not? 189

Low Energy, Low Performance 191

Is There a New Approach to Lane 4 Breathing?..... 192

Dancing on Ice: The Cold-Water Theory 192

Different Stages Bonus Training 197

The Luxury Coach for CEOs: Expert in Performance-Based Speaking and Business Branding 199

Opportunity to Work With Sheena 202

Prologue

Say Yes to be a Corporate Athlete

The Science of a Corporate Athlete is the ideal book to help you position yourself in your business and career. It also offers a distinctive approach to standing out in the present moment.

Are the demands placed on corporate executives more rigorous than those on professional athletes?

Today's corporate world is much like professional sport; it is fiercely competitive, mentally and physically demanding, and requires constant vigilance and training more than ever to maintain health, happiness, and career success. Executives and business professionals must achieve key results quickly.

What if there were a way to learn mastery with a difference? Are you prepared to delve deeper to calibrate your personal and professional performance? Do you wish to build the life you have always dreamed of, with a focus on your lifestyle? Could you commence your self-mastery and leadership programme right now?

In this unique book, Sheena LC Walker serves as a top mentor to CEOs and high achievers who seek business success. As a Global Mark Design Trainer, I will show you how to transition from being an expert to an authority in your field, break performance boundaries, and achieve world-class status both personally and professionally, with the mental preparedness of an Olympic athlete.

Now you are wondering how you can "Win Beyond the Arena."

The Science of a Corporate Athlete illustrates to C-suite executives and business professionals how to thrive within and beyond the corporate sphere.

Drawing parallels between sport and business, Sheena reveals that cultivating self-mastery skills, mentally, physically, and emotionally, provides the CEO with a winning edge. This advantage is vital for establishing a world-class career and business.

Today's challenging business climate requires every top executive to have the grit, determination, and mental preparedness to "Win Beyond the Arena" and become the company of choice.

Say Yes to becoming a Corporate Athlete is the ideal book to help you position yourself in your business and career. It also offers a distinctive approach to standing out in the present moment.

Why would many business professionals want to avoid being top performers now? In my experience within companies, I have observed a notable deficiency in the essential skills required to establish oneself as an authority in the field.

I have been captivated by what distinguishes champions and world-class athletes for thirty years. I was intrigued by the performance of top business experts, so I examined the habits and processes that contributed to their exceptional success. This exploration inspired me to write thirty e-books on performance in the workplace to acquire a competitive edge.

The staff's feedback was outstanding. How can a methodology based on sports performance be so effective in business? What if you could apply these winning strategies to achieve exceptional results in your life and work?

After researching my findings, I devised innovative strategies and a methodology into a Unique Signature Model to help business professionals thrive in a challenging economy, regardless of the circumstances.

Reflecting on my days as an athlete, national coach, and Special Olympics manager, I understand precisely where my grit, determination, discipline, and obsession with mastery, success, and world-class thinking originated. I genuinely know what that success feels like.

What if everything you do leads you to daily podium success and the mastery of these Olympic skills? What might success look like for you as a CEO, an executive, and an entrepreneur in today's dynamic economy?

Would adopting these daily Olympic-winning strategies propel you from the pit lane to the fast track of success? Are you ready to take your position at the starting block? You don't have to be held back any longer. What matters is that, just like a sports coach, I will personally and professionally teach you how to concentrate on your game and become a Corporate Olympian.

Imagine receiving world-class training infused with the spirit of a champion. Can you envision your expertise and standing as you lead the field in the future?

This unique conceptual model addresses eight critical areas for performance improvement.

It has been delivered through workshops, training sessions, and development days, incorporating presentations, public speaking, leadership, self-coaching, and mentoring skills. It follows my distinctive model, employing innovative and creative methods to empower executives to become high performers.

The Podium Performance Booster

Achieving excellent positioning in the business world starts with adequate performance. But how can you become an elite performer in the corporate arena? What does this involve? In this chapter, you will acquire the skills necessary to achieve critical results swiftly, create a winning game plan, and maintain an advantage over your competitors. You will discover the tools to enhance profitability, control costs, and optimise resource allocation across your team.

Explore the winning advantage that distinguishes high achievers from the rest. Embrace a new methodology and cultivate self-mastery that generates a significant impact. Self-mastery is a vital skill for World-class tennis player Andy Murray prior to his retirement trained to give him that Olympic-winning edge. An advantage his competitors cannot foresee. His vision, goals, and aspirations converge to elevate his performance to a world-class standard. The same principle holds true in business.

So why do so many individuals and businesses operate as if they are in a constant state of emergency? The answer lies in a lack of business acumen, a limited understanding of financial data, and a failure to grasp the critical success factors necessary for achieving lasting results. There are no pre-set rules for success, which is an unbelievable yet often true approach to business.

Investing in self-development and honing your skills is essential for growth. Would Andy Murray train as if he were responding to emergencies, rushing through his preparation? I'll leave it to you to answer that. So, why don't you do the same?

Join me, Sheena, on this journey towards self-mastery. You'll develop daily performance habits that will position you as an expert in your field. My step-by-step methodology is designed to help you and your team adopt clear, consistent planning that drives lasting success.

By learning high-level strategies from top business leaders and elite athletes, you can multiply your productivity, elevate your presence in the marketplace, and capture valuable market share. Your journey to podium success starts now.

Learn how to design, develop, deliver, and refine a distinctive business model. Envision positioning your organisation as a world-class brand, delivering impressive results with speed and precision.

Becoming a top performer and recognised expert begins with understanding the success formula used by business champions. Through conceptual modelling, you can strengthen your performance and achieve superior outcomes.

Discover the rules for achieving greatness with our Podium Booster by Design, which allows you to develop your brand voice, identity, profile, and expertise.

Different Stages

Effective speaking is one of the most valuable skills in today's business world. Strong presentation and public speaking abilities are essential for success as a business leader, trainer, or aspiring speaker. Leading companies expect key personnel to excel in communication, think on their feet, engage audiences, and demonstrate impactful skills that set them apart from competitors.

Dale Carnegie's *How to Win Friends and Influence People* highlight the importance of influence, a crucial, yet often overlooked, skill in business education. Influential speakers, though not necessarily born with natural talent, can significantly advance their careers by mastering the art of communication.

This chapter explores why communication and influence are critical.

It illustrates the pitfalls of public speaking by accident, using examples such as Michael Bay's unpreparedness at a Samsung press conference. You will learn the principles of effective public speaking and how to prepare and deliver impactful presentations in any situation.

Effective communication is crucial when aiming for a promotion, starting a new business, or presenting a project. This chapter provides techniques for delivering engaging presentations, managing teams effectively, and establishing yourself as an influential figure within your organisation.

The Art of Infinite Coaching

Have you noticed how the world is evolving? We live in a dynamic economy, and leading the field, acquiring a competitive edge, and becoming the preferred individual and company is increasingly challenging.

Breaking performance boundaries as an executive can be both personally and professionally demanding, and achieving results that propel you to the pinnacle of your potential ranks among the primary goals of executives and business professionals. How are these results achieved? What distinguishes elite performers from the average?

As a young athlete, national coach, and Special Olympics manager, I will never forget the "Peak Performance Pyramid" of coaching and personal development, a model that remains just as relevant today.

My coach, Mr Blair, taught me the importance of mental preparedness, consistent performance, grit, and determination. I remember him once telling me I had foolish habits and would never succeed because I was always busy fixing things.

Let me ask you: Are you still fixing things? You may need to learn new habits.

As I watched the Ryder Cup at Gleneagles, I listened intently to Paul McGinley, the captain. He employed the fast-forward feedback method to assist the players. You might be surprised to learn that he was joined by the most unlikely of performance coaches, Sir Alex Ferguson.

Coaches and players execute plays that their competitors do not foresee. These are two vastly different approaches to achieving world-class coaching performance. What if you were taught to embody an athlete's grit, determination, and mental preparedness? Would you become Olympic fit?

Imagine adopting an efficient and practical mindset similar to that of professional golfers, such as those on the Ryder Cup team. Are you at the peak of your abilities, sitting on a park bench, watching others play, and wishing you could be a standout performer?

What can we learn from peak performers, and what do they do that we can emulate? Daily, they have a performance director; imagine if you had a director in the business world, an experienced, highly trained performance coach who would provide you with the tools, tips, and techniques to achieve successful business strategies.

I have applied my approach to assist business owners with significant financial implications. Sharing my methodology necessitates immediate correction and a new direction. As a corporate athlete, you can execute plays in under 24 hours. Envision using this framework to shift your business from the pit lane to the fast lane. Are you committed, or making excuses?

In today's economy, with self-proclaimed experts flooding the market, it's time to step up. To become the preferred company and employer of choice, we need a competitive edge in everything we undertake. Winning isn't everything; it is the only thing.

In this chapter, I will explain how to become Game-Ready by mastering the principles of High-Performance coaching, a crucial tool for improving performance, productivity, profitability, and results.

The Laser Leadership Archetypes

In today's dynamic economy, exceptional leadership from executives and CEOs is essential for success. This chapter introduces the concept of "Laser Leadership," which requires leaders to have a clear vision, actionable plans, and a deep understanding of key success factors to effectively manage and motivate regional, national, and global teams. Great leaders are characterised by their ability to energise conversations, exert influence, and skilfully manage crises and change.

The chapter critiques the widespread lack of leadership skills seen in many executives and highlights the importance of ongoing development. Using examples such as Jeff Bezos and Steve Jobs, it shows how influential leaders simplify complex processes and strategically position their brands.

Insights from military leadership training underscore the value of decisive and direct leadership, as well as its parallels with effective athlete management. The chapter encourages you to imagine cultivating a high-performing culture and becoming an "Ambassadorial Leader." It provides situational leadership models to enhance your leadership style and effectiveness across various business settings, helping you strengthen your ability to influence, develop talent, and lead with purpose.

The Training Edge Creator

Preparation is essential for success across all fields, whether you are an athlete, musician, executive, or professional in any sector. Champions consistently prepare to achieve success, and this principle applies universally. Excellent companies and their leaders recognise the importance of possessing the right skills and critical success factors to maintain an advantage in a dynamic economy.

This chapter reflects on personal experiences as a young athlete, where mental rehearsal and disciplined training were vital. It shows how such preparation builds confidence and dedication. This discipline, seen in early morning training sessions and a steadfast drive for personal bests, translates naturally into the business world.

The chapter questions whether holding a title or excelling in a specific role exempts individuals from ongoing training. It notes that many senior executives and professionals often overlook opportunities for continual professional development (CPD). The author provides a real-world example of a director whose lack of business training impacted performance, emphasising the importance of ongoing learning in maintaining high standards.

The text discusses criticism regarding high standards and the necessity of mastering training techniques, emphasising how rigorous training fosters expertise and provides a competitive edge. The chapter also addresses performance anxiety, which can impact athletes and business professionals, stressing that structured training can help overcome these challenges.

Ultimately, the chapter advocates for a training mindset, focusing on daily achievements and ongoing personal and professional development. It offers insights and techniques from elite athletes that can be applied to attain world-class results in any field, ensuring that one maintains an expert position and performs at one's best.

Crafting Enchanting Customer Experiences

Exceptional customer service is a vital driver of business success. It often relies on simple, cost-free habits that can have a considerable impact. According to a Moray Poll, the top three habits valued by customers include keeping promises, using "please" and "thank you," and offering a genuine smile. While these actions are simple, they can significantly enhance customer satisfaction and loyalty.

Reflect on your recent customer service interactions. Did you receive feedback? What do clients say about your services? By understanding and implementing essential habits that attract and retain customers, you can make a lasting impression without incurring additional costs.

Creating a memorable customer experience involves more than simply delivering good service. It requires making customers feel valued and providing personalised interactions, encouraging them to share their positive experiences. Companies like BMW and Amazon exemplify this with their just-in-time customer service principles, which afford them a competitive edge and establish high standards in the market.

Nevertheless, inadequate customer service remains a widespread issue. This chapter explores the factors contributing to poor service and the methods for addressing them, arguing that employing world-class performers within your organisation can bring about change. Drawing on experiences at Boots, where exceptional customer service was a key focus, the chapter highlights how comprehensive training and a commitment to service excellence can result in a competitive market position and your business as a market leader.

Through personal anecdotes and insights from companies such as Cap Gemini, the chapter emphasises the significance of mastering customer service skills and cultivating a culture that prioritises exceptional service. By embracing the nine habits outlined, you can grow your brand, foster customer loyalty, and attain a level of service that positions you as a leader in your field.

The Master Mentor Formula

Exceptional mentorship plays a crucial role in enhancing performance and fostering growth across a wide range of sectors, including medicine, finance, sales, and leadership. Influential mentors bring expertise that helps elevate others' skills, supporting career progression and organisational achievement. Mentors can notably enhance staff performance by offering mastery through a unique approach, giving individuals a competitive advantage.

Training, coaching, and mentoring often require clarification in today's business environment, even though each has distinct purposes. Ideally, mentors should play a central role within their organisations; however, many companies lack formal mentoring frameworks, necessitating more structured training and approaches. This contrasts with fields such as medicine, where rigorous standards and quality assurance govern mentoring practices.

Consider the implications if professionals, such as doctors or surgeons, were required to receive better mentorship after completing their formal education. Such scenarios are unacceptable within the medical field; however, similar standards are often absent in business mentoring. This chapter advocates establishing clear mentoring boundaries and guidelines to ensure both effectiveness and professionalism.

The mentoring industry is vast, with many self-proclaimed experts offering varying levels of expertise. To become an exceptional mentor, it is essential to follow six key steps. These focus on sustaining specialist work, building strong relationships, developing human capital, and pushing the limits of performance. Mastering these elements can reshape mindsets, improve outcomes, and drive growth, even in complex environments.

The Prosperity of Wealth and Wellbeing

Successful individuals, including top business leaders and world-class athletes, understand the value of "Quality Recovery" time to recharge and reset. Contrary to the belief that constant effort is essential for success, these individuals embrace a balanced approach, incorporating daily well-being practices into their routines. High achievers such as Robin Sharma, Jeff Bezos, Tony Robbins, Andy Murray, Ronaldo, and Messi use their downtime to focus on mental, physical, and emotional health, demonstrating that strategic recovery is vital to sustained excellence.

This chapter explores how adopting the mindset and routines of elite performers can enhance well-being and professional effectiveness. Self-improvement and well-being are presented as essential components for achieving excellence in any field. Outstanding CEOs and senior professionals often cultivate a calm, composed demeanour, which enables them to engage in persuasive, high-impact conversations and lead with clarity.

Organisations are increasingly recognising the value of structured well-being programmes, which protect staff time, reduce absenteeism, and boost morale. This chapter highlights the importance of avoiding overwork, particularly for senior executives, and the negative effects of excessive media exposure on emotional well-being. Taking breaks from media and creating space for personal reflection can significantly improve both mood and productivity.

Personal anecdotes, such as time spent in a garden shed for mental rejuvenation, illustrate the benefits of stepping away from daily pressures to reset and innovate. Incorporating dedicated retreat time into your schedule can enhance creativity and support a more balanced mindset. The chapter encourages readers to design a well-being routine that promotes calm, reduces clutter, and supports both personal and professional success.

Ultimately, this chapter underscores the importance of integrating well-being practices into everyday life. It offers practical strategies for recentring yourself, embracing quiet moments, and nurturing creative thinking to build a more balanced and fulfilling lifestyle.

Chapter 1
The Podium Performance Booster

"World-class execution begins with world-class planning. Without a script, even the best actor loses the plot."
Sheena Walker

"Success is no accident. It is hard work, perseverance, learning, studying, sacrifice, and most of all, a love of what you are doing or learning to do." Pele

Great Ones Plan with Class

If I mention the word *'success'*, what do you think of immediately? Success for our recent Olympians in Paris meant winning a gold medal and standing on the golden podium of achievement. Would you agree that, as a business professional, achieving podium success and developing winning strategies beyond your business arena would be fantastic?

Reflecting on the Commonwealth Games and the Olympics, what defines athletes as world-class? Every competition has its hero, but behind every gold medal are hours of preparation, planning, and training. A well-organised approach, combined with guidance from a high-quality sports performance coach, motivates athletes to achieve their best, allowing them to execute plays their rivals won't anticipate. What's essential in the business world, just like with a sports coach, is that your business coach helps you focus on your game plan to improve your results.

What Successful People Do Differently

Many people hire personal trainers to help them reach their fitness goals. After all, this level of individual attention costs money. One reason is that an experienced professional can help you maximise the benefits of your gym sessions by providing guidance and motivation to work harder. The same logic applies when working with a career coach as a professional or businessperson.

But stop, wait a minute. Despite the popularity of personal trainers, people can still be seen working out in the gym and running through the parks on their own. They've figured out what to do and taken the initiative to do it. You can apply this self-coaching approach to life, career, and business.

However, to be truly first-class, it's essential to work with a professional. In this chapter, I will outline the steps that athletes and business professionals take to establish themselves as authorities.

Director Note: *Nurture Your Personal and Professional Growth*

From Disruption to Planning with Class

We are in a dynamic economy, and businesses have been challenged by a new reality brought on by COVID-19. No one saw this coming. This is forcing organisations to redesign their business models. However, many lack the knowledge, skills, or experience to do so. The red light is flashing. Businesses have frozen, and, like a deadly disease, complacency has crept into the minds of organisations.

What if there were a green light to do things differently? Move from uncertainty to a powerful opportunity for a business overhaul, like an MOT or engine change, to become more efficient in learning and implementing better systems and processes than your competitors.

Green Light of Obsession

As a former athlete and experienced business leader, I am thrilled to share my passion for excellence that transcends sport and business. Over the years, my journey has been one of exploration as I've investigated the common threads connecting the paths of world-class athletes and accomplished business leaders.

It's fascinating how the principles of excellence in one field often translate into success in another. Athletes and business leaders alike rely on discipline, resilience, goal setting, and the ability to perform under pressure. My research into these similarities could have significant implications for both athletic coaching and business leadership. The rapid feedback I received showed that my findings resonated with professionals and corporate executives, as I uncovered the shared qualities, and differences, between world-class athletes and business experts.

With a background in business, marketing, human resources, and training, and three decades of hands-on experience across various sectors, I recognise that the qualities which drive individuals to greatness are universal. Whether on the field or in the boardroom, these qualities remain constant.

I've explored this topic in depth through extensive research and practical application, culminating in the development of *"Say Yes to becoming a Corporate Athlete Model."* This innovative framework incorporates key performance principles.

This Unique Signature System (USS) covers eight critical areas of performance improvement, offering workshops, training, and development programmes that equip individuals and organisations with the tools needed to excel. From effective communication and leadership development to coaching skills and tailored training, each pillar of performance is designed to foster a culture of excellence.

However, our approach extends beyond that. You will adopt cutting-edge techniques to customise your strategies to meet the ever-changing demands of the workplace. We recognise that success in today's world necessitates adaptability and innovation, and we are dedicated to remaining ahead of the curve.

The goal is straightforward: inspire individuals and teams in your organisations to achieve greatness by consistently doing the right things better. By fostering a passion for performance and providing practical tools for success, you will empower your clients to surpass the competition and realise their full potential.

So, as we embark on this journey together, let us remember: while the rules of success may have changed, the principles of excellence remain the same. By harnessing the power of sports methodology and applying it to the business world, you can unlock a new era of achievement, facing every challenge with confidence, overcoming every obstacle with resilience, and reaching every goal with excellence.

We will examine the critical lessons learned from the Olympic experience and high-performance sport, lessons that apply just as powerfully to business and professional life.

Director Note: *World-Class Wealth Begins with World-Class Thinking*

Successful People Plan with Class

Let's discuss something crucial: having a winning mindset. I bet you've experienced moments of negativity when everything seems to go wrong. Perhaps you think, *"Nobody takes me seriously at work,"* or *"I need to improve my performance, but it seems impossible."* Does this sound familiar?

If you want things to change, you must focus on what is truly important. Consider champions like those in the Ryder Cup or Formula 1. They don't merely aim for average; they strive to be the best. And do you know what they do? They take risks. They plan meticulously to outperform their opponents, always aiming for victory.

Let me ask: are you willing to go that extra mile? Are you hungry for success, both personally and professionally? It's time to step up and make your competitors play catch-up. Become the authority in your field and start achieving those key results, fast.

Here's a little secret: keep your plans under wraps. Confidentiality gives you the element of surprise, allowing you to stay one step ahead of the game.

Director Note: *Decisions, Decisions, Decisions Take Ownership*

Be the Greatest Showman

It's all about stepping out of your comfort zone and embracing the role of the greatest showman in your organisation. Picture yourself as the professional performer who owns the stage and commands attention.

What kind of results do you think you'd achieve with that mindset?

In my experience, there's a noticeable difference between those who strive for excellence and those who settle for mediocrity, whether in the corporate world or the public sector. And let me tell you, I know which group I'd rather belong to.

In *The Little Book of Coaching*, Ken Blanchard and Don Shula hit the nail on the head when they said, *"A broad target that's easy to achieve leads to the 'puddle' of mediocrity."* So, clearly defining your goal is essential. This clarity is a powerful motivator, helping you stay focused and committed, even when the going gets tough.

High achievers don't just wait for success; they actively set themselves up for it by regularly reviewing their progress. Evaluated reflection turns experience into insight, paving the way for growth and improvement.

Take a page from Tony Robbins' book: track your accomplishments and magic moments like you're saving receipts for tax purposes. Regular reviews of your business, career, life, and finances allow you to identify core principles and make informed decisions about what to do next.

Director Note: *Champions Develop World-Class Beliefs Before They Become Champions*

A Giant Life Starts with Giant-Class Thinking

Let's talk about the class of thinking you operate in. Have you considered whether you're thinking in economy, business, or first-class terms?

If you're in economy class, you might have a basic understanding of your industry. However, you could be limiting yourself by not fully grasping the core principles of business acumen. Conversely, if you're in business class, you've likely gained knowledge, skills, and experience, but you may find it difficult to craft a strategy that truly works for you. It's common to feel overwhelmed, jumping from project to training to any course you can access, only to find yourself buried in what I call "brain clutter."

Now, picture this: what if you could elevate your thinking to a first-class level? What would that look like? It's about demonstrating a standard of quality in every aspect of your business, becoming a model of good practice, and setting the bar high for yourself and your team.

But where do you start? Do you need a compelling reason to transform your business and differentiate yourself?

Consider this: we encounter people of varying levels, average, sound, outstanding, and some exceptional individuals who consistently outshine the competition. The question is, are you commercially viable? Are you willing to embrace a service that delivers outstanding results, or will you settle for being average?

As a director, I challenge you to assess your current state. Are you caged in old habits, comfortable in your routine, or charged with the energy to evolve? Can you rise to the challenge and develop giant-class thinking? It is time to break free from limitations and reach new heights of success. Let's make it happen!

Director Note: *Are You Caged, Comfortable, or Charged?*

Does Your Class Allow You to Go the Extra Mile?

Having a Ferrari in my living room might sound unusual, but it serves as a powerful reminder every morning. Standing on the track at Monza, the home of Ferrari in Milan, I reflected on how I could match the performance metrics of a Ferrari driver. When you think of Ferrari, you think of world-class performance and leadership. Imagine embodying that level of excellence in your endeavours. What can we learn from Ferrari about performance, and how can we apply those principles to excel in the first-class lane?

Winning extends beyond the track; it's about being an expert in your industry and positioning yourself as the go-to person, thereby gaining a competitive edge in everything you do. It's about becoming a corporate ambassador, representing excellence in every aspect.

At Performance by Design, we have a unique approach to performance. What inspires me? Well, every morning, as soon as my feet hit the ground, I'm greeted by my Ferrari. I visualise the five Ps of performance. Is it normal? Perhaps not, but it's different, and it mentally prepares me to lead the field. Imagine if everyone had their own visual Ferrari in their lounge. How might that propel us from the pit lane to the fast track in our businesses?

So, why are we faced with challenges in achieving performance excellence? The world has evolved, and so must we. The landscape today is vastly different from what it was a decade ago.

We are witnessing explosive growth in social media, online shopping, technological breakthroughs, global economic shifts, and significant changes in consumer behaviour.

Today, relying on outdated performance methods is no longer enough. The old career escalator is jammed, and businesses are grappling with a new reality. Recent global events have brought unprecedented disruptions, affecting markets worldwide and causing widespread unemployment, insolvency, and business collapse. It is clear: to survive in this new era, we must adapt, innovate, and redefine what it means to excel.

Director Note: *Stay Ahead of the Competition by Creating Competence*

Could You Plan Your Winning Performance the Ferrari Way?

The epitome of world-class is transitioning from the pit lane to the fast track, eventually reaching podium success. It's all about meticulous preparation, strategic planning, and relentless practice with precision, much like Ferrari drivers who walk every inch of the track, inch by inch, ensuring they're fully prepared for the race ahead.

Operating a commercially viable and sustainable business is like running a finely tuned machine. When all cylinders are in sync and working at peak levels, your exposure increases, credibility strengthens, and your business grows steadily. People invest in your products, programmes, and services, making your income steady and robust.

However, just like a finely tuned machine, when one area of your business falls out of alignment, it affects the overall efficiency and performance of the entire organisation. That's why it's crucial to regularly assess your business's health and identify areas that may need fine-tuning. By asking the right questions and addressing issues promptly, you can ensure that your business continues to operate optimally.

Remember, winning isn't everything, it's the only thing. Strive for excellence in every aspect of your business, and success will follow.

Director Note: *Be Obsessed with Victory and Performance*

How Can You Win Beyond the Arena?

Winning beyond the arena involves breaking down your critical goals into manageable steps and assigning specific time limits to prevent procrastination. It's essential to set realistic yet slightly ambitious deadlines, ones that stretch your boundaries without becoming overwhelming. Documenting your goals brings clarity, allowing you to track progress, reflect on milestones achieved, and make adjustments where needed.

To propel yourself forward, embrace actions that push you beyond your comfort zone. Give yourself permission to take calculated risks, recognising that fear or failure often impose the only real limitations in life. Visualise a scenario where fear is absent and your belief in success is unshakable. This mindset inspires bold action and, in turn, drives powerful outcomes.

By adopting a proactive approach, you can achieve both personal and professional growth. Seize opportunities that align with your ambitions and dismantle the barriers that may have limited your potential. With determination and courage, you can attain success beyond the confines of the arena, reaching new heights and realising your most important objectives.

Director Note: *Champion Authority to Achieve Greatness*

Nothing Changes Until Your Mission Becomes Your Obsession

It is essential to ensure that what you choose to pursue is something you genuinely care about and wish to achieve. Without true passion and desire, you are likely to lack the motivation to follow through with your goals.

Sometimes, we hold back due to self-doubt or fear of failure. If you find yourself hesitating or lacking self-belief, try the following exercise:

First, reflect on how you typically react, feel, and think when worried or uncertain. Pay attention to your body language, thoughts, and emotions in these moments.

Next, think about how you react, feel, and think when you are confident of success. Notice the stark differences between these two states, they are usually quite apparent.

Now, visualise your new intention or goal. As you do this, consciously breathe, stand, and speak as you would when you are sure of success. By embodying your goal, you can achieve it with renewed conviction and resolve.

Embodying confidence and determination can help shift your mindset from doubt and hesitation to belief and decisiveness. This can empower you to overcome obstacles and pursue your aspirations with greater clarity and purpose.

Director Note: *Mental Preparedness Is a Discipline of Champions*

Risk More Than Is Required to Be a Class Performer

The words of my swimming coach still resonate with me today, constantly reminding me of the importance of wholehearted commitment to achieving our goals.

Say Yes

I recall vividly those early mornings at the poolside, the dim light barely piercing through the darkness as I went through my pre-training rituals. Mr Blair, my coach, was a formidable presence, his voice commanding attention even in the stillness of the morning.

One particular morning stands out vividly in my memory. As I stood at the pool's edge, hesitating before dipping my toe into the water, Mr Blair's voice sliced through the silence like a thunderclap.

"Sheena, just what are you doing?" he exclaimed, his tone sharp with disbelief.

"I'm just dipping my toe in the water," I replied sheepishly, uncertain of his reaction.

He shook his head sternly and retorted, "Sheena, if you want to be an elite performer, stop toe-dipping and testing all the time."

His words hit me like a wave crashing against the shore. In that moment, I understood his message. Success wasn't about tiptoeing around challenges or hesitating at the water's edge, it was about diving in with unwavering commitment and determination.

From that day forward, I approached my training with a newfound resolve. No longer content with toe-dipping, I plunged into each session with full intensity, pushing myself to the limit and striving for excellence in every stroke.

Now, I ask you: are you developing your mindset and achieving your personal best daily? Are you ready for action, or are you still holding back?

Let Mr Blair's words serve as a reminder to embrace challenges wholeheartedly and dive into the deep end of life's pool with courage and determination. That is how we achieve greatness.

Directors Note: *Successful People Have Successful Daily Habits*

When You Hit a Boulder, Bounce Back

Obstacles are a natural part of any journey, but how we respond to them determines our success. It's easy to feel discouraged and give up when faced with challenges, but history is filled with examples of individuals who persisted through adversity and achieved greatness.

Take Colonel Sanders, for instance. At 65, he achieved his dream of creating Kentucky Fried Chicken. Despite being rejected 1,009 times when trying to sell his chicken recipe, he persevered until he heard his first "yes."

Then there's Walt Disney, who faced rejection 302 times before securing financing for his dream of creating Disneyland. Despite numerous setbacks, he remained steadfast in his vision and eventually built "the happiest place on earth."

These stories serve as powerful reminders that obstacles are not roadblocks but opportunities for growth and resilience. Instead of seeing them as signs to give up, we should view them as challenges to overcome on the path to our dreams.

So, the next time you encounter a challenge, resist the urge to give up on your goals. Draw inspiration from those who have gone before you, and choose to leave a legacy for others to follow. Remember: success is not defined by the absence of obstacles, but by our ability to overcome them.

Director Note: *Keep Digging till You Find that Vein of Gold*

Is Your Work a Craft or Class Act?

Transforming your work into a class act requires an understanding of performance coaching principles and the ability to apply them to your challenges. Although a performance coach may assist with significant issues, many minor problems can be addressed independently by using a similar approach.

Begin by clarifying your desires and transforming them into a design-thinking intention. This entails clearly defining your goals and objectives while ensuring they align with your values and aspirations. Once you have a clear vision, identify and prioritise the actions required to achieve your goals. Be passionate and persistent in pursuing these actions, staying committed to your objectives despite challenges.

Successful individuals often follow these steps, whether or not they are consciously aware of it. Those committed to enhancing their lives recognise the significance of setting clear goals, taking consistent action, and persevering in the pursuit of their dreams. Conversely, those who neglect these principles often find themselves trapped in old patterns and confronted with the same unsatisfying outcomes.

Ultimately, you owe it to yourself to pursue what truly matters to you. Choose meaningful and compelling goals that ignite your passion and drive you to work towards them every day. By remaining committed and focused on your objectives, you can make a significant difference in your life and draw closer to realising your dreams.

Director Note: *Elevate Your Ideas into a First-Class Act*

Could You Lead the Field in a New Market?

David Williams from *Forbes* magazine presents a compelling argument about the necessity for businesses to adopt the mindset of Corporate Athletes. While not filling stadiums, the strategy of planning and training for success, as seen in the sporting world, could have a transformative effect on our economy.

Imagine the impact of UK business leaders studying the strategies of top sports stars and applying them to their teams. The recent summer of sporting events, including the Tokyo Olympics, perfectly showcased dedication, resilience, and performance excellence. Businesses could learn valuable lessons from these top achievers and transfer their techniques to their staff.

With a background in competitive swimming and coaching, and now as a Corporate Global Trainer and international public speaker on human performance, I passionately believe in the power of applying sports principles to business success.

Avoiding the admission of running or managing a failing or underperforming business requires a shift in mindset. Instead of blaming external factors such as poor staff performance or market difficulties, it is essential to take ownership of the situation. Success or failure ultimately begins with the business owner, director, manager, or HR professional.

Simple strategies inspired by professional athletes can help businesses unlock the full potential of their workforce. By fostering a culture of dedication, resilience, and performance excellence, companies can overcome challenges and achieve remarkable success. It is time to take a page from the playbook of top sports stars and transform our approach to business performance.

Director Note: *Does Corporate Excellence Sustain the Competitive Edge?*

Inspire Others Through a Winning Environment

Success, both personally and professionally, is multifaceted and goes beyond simply completing tasks or supporting staff. It encompasses achieving mastery in one's endeavours, making a meaningful impact, and continually striving for improvement.

To me, success is about self-mastery and personal growth. It centres on pushing boundaries, challenging myself to improve each day, and achieving greatness in whatever I pursue. I incorporate methodologies from various fields, including sports, into my professional life to mentor and develop entrepreneurs and leaders.

Reflecting on the performances of athletes like Andy Murray, Adam Peaty, and Duncan Scott can help us gain insights into the critical elements of success. These elite performers achieve remarkable results by adhering to performance plans tailored to their goals and challenges.

Central to their success is a 'Game Plan': a strategic approach that guides their training, preparation, and execution. Although each athlete may have different objectives, they all concentrate on a formula that distinguishes them as champions.

It is worth noting that athletes and musicians rarely discuss 'goals' in the traditional sense. Instead, they focus on the process, the journey, and their daily commitment to excellence. This mindset shift is crucial for achieving sustained success and becoming experts in their respective fields.

Director Note: *Champions Develop World-Class Beliefs Before They Become Champions*

Is Your Corporate World Like the World of Professional Sports?

Imagine a world where the strategies of world-class athletes are not confined solely to the sports arena but are unleashed in the realm of business. Picture yourself standing at the podium of success, with the winning edge that propels you to greatness.

In today's fiercely competitive landscape, where mental and physical demands are at an all-time high, we must approach our careers with the same intensity and dedication as elite athletes. Just as athletes meticulously train their bodies and minds, we must cultivate the same commitment and discipline in our professional endeavours.

So, who is your role model in the business world? Who inspires you to push beyond your limits and strive for excellence? Imagine tapping into their strategies and insights to elevate your performance.

Successful musicians and business professionals share a common trait: they don't settle for mediocrity. They understand that mastery requires constant vigilance, relentless practice, and a willingness to embrace challenges head-on.

However, it's not just about competition; it's about creating an engaging and captivating product that resonates with audiences and leaves a lasting impression. Embodying expertise, excellence, and emotional connection is the best way to build a winning business.

Now, more than ever, as uncertainty looms and doubts creep in, it's time to break through those barriers and reach new heights of success. It's time to embark on the journey of mastery, where proficiency is not merely a prelude but a promise.

So, let's reflect on how athletes break performance boundaries. Let's study their strategies, mindsets, and relentless pursuit of greatness. Then, let's apply those same principles to our own lives and careers.

There will be challenges, and moments of doubt and fear, but with the right mindset, strategy, and support, we can overcome them.

So that we can achieve something significant, let's commit to maximising our performance levels both inside and outside the corporate world. Let's push ourselves beyond our limits and strive for excellence in everything we do. When we do, we'll find ourselves standing on that podium of success, with the world at our feet.

Director Note: *Embark on the Journey of Champions with Great Expectations*

Three DNA Strategies of Champions Determined to Win

How can the best of the best, the elite of the elite, continue improving their performance once their talent and skills are already pushed to the limit? The answer is that they must continually strive to develop their talent and skills and train to bring them to life. Let's look at three principles.

1. Vision and Outcome

Describe in your own words what you're trying to achieve. Make it as concrete as possible so that you'll know when you've accomplished it.

2. High-Performance Goals

Justify the stages on your journey: the things you'll need to improve, and all the barriers you must overcome to achieve your goal.

3. Process Goals

These are the practical tasks you need to complete to achieve high performance. They should produce high-quality output and be transformational.

What are five Self-Mastery questions to ask yourself?

- Will your goals win you an Oscar?
- Are you driven to achieve more?
- Are you still chasing that winning goal?
- Do people tell you this can't be done?
- Do you have an obsession with success?

How have you strategised in the past? What if you had the mind of an athlete who breaks down every technique and analyses every movement? What if you approached your business in the same way?

Your primary goal needs to be both concise and specific. For instance, in business, you might aim to earn £75,000 a year or achieve £1 million in sales revenue. Note that I mentioned sales revenue, I didn't simply say "make", because I was being specific. What if you could become one per cent better at everything you do?

Asking yourself better questions will yield exceptional results, greater success, increased financial gain, and a higher quality of life. Success will place you on the winning stage, but winning will put you at centre stage. The ability to win resides within us all, whether it's the first championship, that first million, a new business, a new idea, or a new direction.

Winning with High-Performance Goals

Winning in business is more demanding than being an athlete governed by timekeepers, referees, guidelines, and rules. How can you win that battle in your mind? Our aim is to achieve a significant goal that benefits your business.

The next step is to break the goal down into four major moves that need to happen. Each move is a project consisting of deliverables, deadlines, and activities that contribute to achieving that million.

Process Goals

You can't go back. You can only look ahead, taking one more step at a time. Become an edger, don't let someone else push you off the mountain.

Plan That New Product, Service or Idea

These are the practical tasks you must undertake to enhance your performance. They should be high quality and transformational in nature.

- **Step One**

  Can you see how simple the moves are? They're big and bold for 12 weeks, but here's the point.

  If you concentrate on creating a product for the first 12 weeks and then selling it for the remainder of the year, you'll stay aligned with your primary goals as long as you remain focused on all other aspects. Does that mean everything will be perfect and go exactly as planned? Probably not, but you will now have a clear focus.

- **Step Two**

  When considering your major moves, highlight the one you're working on and think about what you could achieve in the next 12 weeks. This may require brainstorming. The order and priority don't matter; space it out on a separate piece of paper if you need more room.

- **Step Three**

  With your next move in mind, select the two or three action items that will have the greatest impact on your business, and include them in the first section of the 12-week target.

I'll share that some of my habits were less than perfect during my sporting journey, and my coach roasted me for it. I quickly began to understand what high performers do and realised I needed greater mental preparedness, grit, and determination to plan and train effectively. Why is this often lacking in the business arena?

Every game has its hero, but behind every celebration lie hours of hard work, relentless mental focus, mental toughness, and perseverance. During challenging times, I'll share strategies for overcoming obstacles and how you can quickly get back on track. Refer to the attached template, where you'll see these strategies laid out step by step. I'll also highlight specific challenges that may arise on your business journey so you can prepare for them and explore alternative approaches.

Raise Your Ambitions

Mr Blair's comments during my morning routine took me by surprise. Although his words may have been harsh, the underlying message about the importance of cultivating successful habits and being mindful of one's actions is vital.

When modelling yourself on great people, consider individuals who inspire you in your field or areas where you wish to grow. Whether they're successful entrepreneurs, accomplished athletes, visionary leaders, or others, examine their habits, mindsets, and approaches to challenges.

For instance, if you admire the discipline and focus of a particular athlete, you might emulate their dedication to training and their capacity to remain committed to their goals. If you're in business, consider successful entrepreneurs who've established thriving companies through innovation and perseverance.

Recognising your strengths and areas for improvement is also essential. While it's natural to have habits that might not serve you well, this presents an opportunity for growth and self-awareness. Reflect on which habits you wish to cultivate to support your goals and aspirations. Remember, success is a journey, and it's acceptable to stumble along the way, as long as you keep moving forward and learning from your experiences.

Mr Blair's coaching style was intense and unconventional. While his methods might seem harsh and confusing, there's a method to his madness. Using the clipboard as a visual tool to represent critical areas, such as mindset, performance, and personal best, he emphasised the importance of tracking and improving these aspects of training.

Although his approach can be abrasive, there's significant value in his focus on measurement and monitoring. Keeping track of your mindset, performance metrics, and personal bests enables you to identify your strengths and areas requiring improvement. This allows for a more targeted approach to your development, resulting in better outcomes.

Director Note: *Are You a Clipboard Dummy or a Strategy Board?*

Peak Performance Pyramid

How can we transition from being a clipboard dummy to becoming brilliant? That metaphorical clap on the head reminded me daily to perform at a high level.

Could you imagine Jeff Bezos of Amazon implementing a new strategy, taking a bit of a risk, but failing to monitor progress, evaluate results, or change direction when needed? Correction plus a new direction = brilliant results. Fail to do this, and you'll hit boulders every day.

Beat the Boulders with Bounce-Back-Ability

In the world of sports, athletes frequently encounter obstacles. It often feels as though a boulder is blocking the entire road. Have you experienced a similar situation in business?

I remember attending some crucial trials, returning home, and sharing the experience with my parents. I was surprised that their enthusiasm didn't match my own.

When we hit a stumbling block, such as a "boulder," we have to look at other options, perhaps it's time to seek new opportunities and a fresh direction in business. J.K. Rowling was turned down twelve times while trying to get a book published, but she never gave up. Is that you?

Habitual Excellence Behaviours

As I grew up and entered the working world, I became obsessed with what distinguishes a high achiever from a champion. Observing individuals in the business realm and studying their habits and processes helped me understand how to achieve excellence. I soon realised that, to accomplish anything worthwhile in your career, you must become valuable through personal development.

I began researching what makes individuals world-class in both the sporting and music realms, while also examining those in business. Did they possess similar personality traits and skills? This exploration led me to write 24 e-books focused on business performance to help gain a competitive edge.

Director Note: *Do Your Habits Have an Impact on Your Performance?*

Scorecard of Critical Success

After studying and learning about the world of sports and business, and what made certain individuals and organisations stand out, I developed strategies, habits, and processes into a unique signature model: *The Science of a Corporate Athlete*. I'm proud that this model has instigated change by providing a complete business solution.

When discussing our current economy, David Williams of *Forbes* magazine asked, "What if we had organisations filled with corporate athletes? Imagine organisations with the mind of an athlete."

World-class elite performers discuss mental preparedness, performance, and achieving personal bests every day. I was astonished to discover that these winning sports strategies could be utilised to gain a competitive edge in business, producing remarkable results.

How can you apply these critical success factors of performance in your business?

Conversations among elite athletes always begin with preparation, planning, and training schedules. Imagine if you, like an athlete, questioned yourself daily about your performance, strategy, market presence, and positioning in your business. What if, right now, nothing seems to be working?

Director Note: *Are You Pursuing the Podium Journey to Excellence?*

The Shambles Sheet: When Nothing's Working, and You Don't Know Why

Reflecting on our performance, we should consider adopting better habits, routines, and a strategic direction. Perhaps you have a disorganised sheet that requires immediate attention; a shambles sheet can have severe consequences and lead to a lack of personal and professional direction.

How does one create a dysfunctional team that fails to share the same vision and values?

Some years ago, Steve Redgrave, Captain of the GB rowing team, was obsessed with performance and results. He stated that it took ten years to reach podium gold. Reflecting on his team's performance years later, he identified why it took so long: ten world-class individuals may not be in total harmony or share a unified vision. Communicating your vision and values for measurable success is essential in creating a high-performing team. How can we accomplish this through fast-forward feedback?

Fast-Forward Feedback

Why do those at the top of their game receive fast-tracked feedback from their performance coach to maximise their potential? Feedback is the breakfast of champions, and top athletes alike. Act on feedback immediately, not in a week, a month, or a year.

Do you need to enhance your business by providing actionable feedback? Would Andy Murray hold a coaching session today and continue with the same approach he took last week? That would never happen. Imagine applying these principles in the business world. Why is elite performance so often lacking in business today?

Unintended Leadership: The Accidental CEO Phenomenon

CEOs may sometimes be perceived as accidental leaders or as lacking essential performance planning skills for various reasons. Often, they rise through the ranks due to expertise in a specific area but lack adequate leadership training, resulting in gaps in strategic planning and performance management. Additionally, the dynamic nature of the role requires a diverse skill set, and not all individuals possess expertise in every aspect necessary for effective leadership.

It's important to note that not all CEOs fit into this category. Many possess extensive planning skills and strategic foresight, driving their organisations towards success. However, CEOs can face challenges due to the evolving demands of their roles and a lack of ongoing professional development.

Become a daily student and invest in continuous learning, mentorship, and support to enhance your professional performance planning capabilities significantly.

Director Note: *Don't Be an Accidental CEO With Serious Implications*

As every exceptional production begins with a solid script, so too does your success begin with structured planning. Step into the role of Director now with these final cues.

Director Note

Chapter 1: Planning with Precision

- True leaders don't just plan they direct the vision. This chapter was your call sheet: the scene is set, the vision is clear, and it's time to act with executive intent.

- Define your ultimate performance goal in one line.

- Eliminate one task that doesn't support your podium success.

- Choose one system to simplify your workflow.

- Schedule a "Director Day" for focused planning every month.

Sheena

Say YES to Performing at the Top

Chapter 2
Different Stages of Speaking

"Your voice is more than sound its strategy. Speak to direct, not to impress." Sheena Walker

Professional speaking is vital in our economy for several reasons, especially for entrepreneurs, leaders, and business professionals. It enhances every aspect of business operations, from strategy and leadership to sales and relationship management. Commercial viability relies on factors such as product quality, market demand, and financial management; effective communication is a crucial enabler that supports and amplifies these components.

To win business investments, professionals must effectively deliver their vision, ideas, and plans to investors, partners, and customers. A clear and compelling presentation can secure funding and attract critical stakeholders. Leaders must be able to articulate their strategies, inspire their teams, and build consensus. Effective communication helps align team efforts, drives organisational goals, and can be the difference between securing business and handing it over to a competitor.

Dale Carnegie wrote *How to Win Friends and Influence People*. This book became a bestseller because the essential skills of influence, relationship building, and trust are rarely taught in the business world, schools, or universities. The ability to influence and persuade others is vital in the business environment. Persuasive communication is essential when negotiating deals, selling products, or driving organisational change.

Change agents can effectively promote their ideas, making it easier to gain support and achieve their goals.

If brand and reputation management are crucial in reflecting a business's values, why is it so essential for senior executives to develop the skills necessary to become exceptional speakers? Being an effective public speaker enhances both personal and organisational reputation, establishing credibility and authority in one's field. Public appearances, media interactions, and speaking engagements provide opportunities to reinforce brand values and messaging.

While commercial viability depends on various factors, professional speaking plays a crucial role in marketing and sales efforts. Effectively communicating a product or service's value proposition can profoundly influence sales and customer acquisition. For entrepreneurs, a well-delivered pitch can be the difference between securing funding and missing out on opportunities.

Leaders must communicate changes effectively in a rapidly evolving business environment to ensure smooth transitions. This involves managing crises in the boardroom, addressing uncertainties, and guiding teams through transformations. Resilient communication helps maintain morale and productivity during challenging times.

Have you noticed that the world of work is undergoing significant changes? Advancing to the next level in your career requires the skills to communicate your message clearly and deliver an impactful presentation during recruitment and selection processes. This is a skill companies increasingly demand from their key personnel to position and command their brand effectively.

In this chapter, I will help you enhance your speaking skills. Have you long desired to become a dynamic, confident, charismatic, and influential speaker? Don't allow negativity or a lack of speaking skills to hold you back.

Director Note: *Speak Up, Scale Up, The Untapped Business Booster*

Is Speaking a Natural Talent?

My journey into public speaking began with intensive training at The Public Speakers University under the guidance of Andy Harrington, one of my current mentors in the pursuit of excellence. I served as an Academy Coach Executive alongside Andy Harrington at his Public Speaking Academy. I now travel worldwide to mentor CEOs and leaders, helping them achieve excellence.

I can still remember the anticipation of my first big conference in front of an audience of 200 people. The ability to inspire and influence delegates to step up and be extraordinary through my speaking was a fantastic experience. Every day, I ask myself how I can become an elite performer and achieve remarkable things to gain recognition, rewards, and success in my career.

I surround myself with genuinely inspirational people who have been there, done that, and worn the T-shirt. This has resulted in significant improvements in my performance. The characteristics of an elite performer and public speaker include authenticity, inspiration, humour, creativity, and genuine passion for what they do.

Throughout my career, I have recognised the importance of continuous learning and personal development. Interacting with leading professionals and thought leaders has allowed me to enhance my skills and expand my horizons. This exposure has provided me with diverse perspectives and innovative methods, enabling me to deliver engaging and impactful speeches.

Mentoring CEOs and leaders worldwide has been a transformative experience. I have witnessed first-hand the significant impact that effective communication can have on leadership and organisational success. By helping leaders articulate their vision and connect with their teams, I contribute to fostering more dynamic and resilient organisations.

One key lesson I have learned is the power of storytelling. Sharing personal anecdotes and real-life examples makes my messages more relatable and memorable. They help bridge the gap between the speaker and the audience, fostering a deeper connection and engagement.

As I continue to evolve in my career, I focus on pushing the boundaries of what is possible in public speaking. I am committed to exploring new techniques, technologies, and platforms to enhance my presentations and reach a wider audience. My aim is to inspire and empower others to unlock their full potential and achieve extraordinary success.

In summary, my journey into public speaking has been characterised by rigorous training, valuable mentorship, and a relentless pursuit of excellence. By remaining authentic, inspirational, humorous, creative, and genuine, I strive to leave a lasting impact on every audience I address. Public speaking is not merely a profession for me; it is a passion and a calling that I wholeheartedly embrace.

Director Note: *Speakers Are Not Born; They Are Shaped and Trained*

Commanding the Room: From Page to Stage

Professional speaking is not merely about delivering a message; it is about connecting with your audience on a deeper, more meaningful level. It requires continuous learning, adaptability, and a commitment to excellence. These principles have shaped my journey in public speaking, guiding me to evolve and refine my skills consistently.

The lessons I have learned as an athlete and sports coach are invaluable. The discipline, teamwork, and resilience required in sports translate effortlessly into the business world. By applying these principles, I assist leaders and organisations in achieving peak performance. This approach has proven successful across various contexts, from fundraising to corporate training.

When I started giving presentations to raise funds for the Special Olympics, I quickly realised the importance of clarity and passion in communication. My ability to connect with diverse audiences and highlight the significance of my cause was vital in gaining support. Building relationships with local councils, Rotary clubs, and businesses required authenticity and consistent follow-up, demonstrating my commitment to my athletes.

"What you do with little, you do with a lot" resonates deeply with me. It emphasises the importance of consistency and excellence, irrespective of audience size. Every speaking opportunity, whether big or small, is a chance to refine your message and impact lives. This mindset has driven my success and ongoing improvement as a speaker and coach.

Another pivotal moment was my experience at Boots the Chemist during a recruitment campaign. It highlighted the importance of character and reputation. Developing a professional identity that reflects quality, expertise, and integrity is crucial. This experience reinforced that personal growth and professional excellence are intertwined, shaping how I approach every speaking engagement.

In summary, my public speaking journey serves as a testament to the power of continuous growth, genuine connections, and applying sports principles to business. By embracing these elements, I endeavour to inspire and empower others, leaving a lasting impact on every audience I address.

Director Note: *Kick New Doors Wide Open, Personally and Professionally*

My Future in the World of Performance

Reflecting on my days in the chorus of amateur dramatics and my performances on stage, I realise how those experiences shaped my speaking skills. We became great storytellers, commanding the audience's attention with our voices, theatrical principles, body language, and gestures. But the most crucial part was crafting a story to deliver a memorable message. This art of storytelling, combined with the technical skills of performance, forms the foundation of world-class speaking.

Have you ever had a dream? One of my goals was to study theatrical performance, voice modulation, scheduling, radio presenting, television, and the world of film and theatre. That dream led me to the auditorium as an adult student studying film and media at the University of Stirling. My professional life was taking a different direction as I immersed myself in this new realm. Little did I know how soon I would apply my skills to developing world-class speaking programmes.

The principles of theatre and performance are directly applicable to public speaking. Crucial skills include effectively using one's voice, modulating tone and pace, and employing body language and gestures to enhance a message. I honed these techniques in amateur dramatics and later refined them through formal education in film and media.

Studying at the University of Stirling was a transformative experience. The curriculum included a range of subjects, such as voice training and performance techniques, as well as the intricacies of radio and television presenting. Each class contributed a new layer of understanding and competence, equipping me with versatile skills for my speaking engagements.

One of the most valuable lessons I learned was the importance of authenticity. In both acting and public speaking, authenticity resonates with the audience. People can sense when a speaker is genuine and passionate, and this connection makes a presentation memorable. My time studying theatre and media reinforced the importance of being true to oneself and one's message.

The study of film and media also introduced me to the power of visual storytelling. In today's digital age, integrating multimedia elements into a presentation can significantly enhance its impact. Whether through compelling visuals, video clips, or interactive elements, these tools help create a more engaging and immersive experience for the audience.

As I continue to develop my world-class speaking programmes, I draw on the diverse experiences and skills I have gained. My combination of theatrical training, performance techniques, and media studies allows me to deliver informative, captivating, and inspiring presentations. I aim to help others unlock their potential as speakers by applying the core principles of storytelling, authenticity, and multimedia integration.

Director Note: *Are You a Presenter or a Performer in Business?*

Mic Drop Moments That Drive Business Results

Are you a business professional or a leader? In today's competitive arena, performance skills are essential. The ability to stand up and communicate your message effectively is a vital skill that companies expect their key personnel to possess.

Why is it essential to think on your feet and engage the listener during an interview or sales presentation?

The ability to do so can mean the difference between securing a new business deal or job and losing it to a competitor. Without excellent communication skills and proficiency in English, this can pose a serious challenge. Would you agree that one must be commercially viable in various business contexts?

Who needs to hear this? Perhaps you are a business professional or CEO looking to advance your career. You aim to position yourself as an expert or authority and devise new strategies to make your performance memorable and achieve credible results.

All this sounds perfect, but consider this: audience research indicates that 77% of the population, according to Dr Michael DiGiorgio, experiences public speaking anxiety, which can affect their careers and lifestyles. Have you ever felt this way? What if you could move from the pit lane to the fast track? Would this make you more profitable?

Director Note: *Step up to the Starting Block of* **Profitability**

Stellar Speaking Skills in the Corporate World

Senior executives and directors who seek out performance coaches typically do so because they are dissatisfied with a specific aspect of their public speaking abilities. They feel they're not impactful and that their business message, full of facts and information, is often poorly understood and, quite frankly, boring.

Clients frequently inquire about how I began, how I deliver my services effectively, how I ensure I'm easily understood, and how I acquire new business.

When you think about a celebrity rock band like Take That, what comes to mind is red carpet treatment, brilliant music, and expertise in the music industry that makes you go "WOW." Would you agree that thinking like a celebrity rock star would be a fantastic place to start in becoming a dynamic, confident, and influential speaker? For many business professionals, the red carpet feels out of reach.

Effective communication is vital for success in recruitment and selection, career development, the boardroom, chairing meetings, and securing new contracts. To become a standout speaker, you must apply five essential core skills:

- **One: Engage the Audience.** Captivate your audience with an engaging story and relatable examples. Do not merely list facts and figures.

- **Two: Be Clear and Concise.** Ensure your message is clear and easily understood. Simplify complex information and avoid jargon.

- **Three: Exude Confidence.** Present yourself with confidence. This can be developed through practice and constructive feedback.

- **Four: Think Like a Rockstar.** Adopt a mindset of excellence and charisma. Strive for a performance that leaves a lasting impression.

- **Five: Practise Authenticity.** Be genuine and authentic in your delivery. Audiences connect better with speakers who are real and passionate.

Director Note: *In summary, by refining these skills, business professionals can enhance their speaking abilities, become more engaging and impactful, and ultimately attain significant career success.*

Do You Lack These Four Performance Skills?

- One: Lack of Expertise Positioning. Many business professionals lack the mastery required for effective presentations. Would Andy Murray step onto the court without honing his skills? Of course not. He is a world-class tennis player who demonstrates his talent at every event. In a crowded market, lacking expertise and visibility relegates you to amateur status.

- Two: Lack of a Signature System. Many speakers lack a signature system. They rely on improvisation, functioning as accidental speakers who hope for the best. This approach undermines business credibility. Would a dentist or surgeon operate without a system in place? Certainly not, as it would create chaos. A structured approach is essential for consistent and reliable outcomes.

- Three: Communication Consistency. Business professionals seeking to enhance their position and influence within their field require consistency. This involves incorporating business language into their organisation's structure, social media, and all forms of communication. Without this consistency, the business model risks becoming fragmented and inefficient.

- Four: No Mentor, Gap in Professional Development. Having a mentor provides valuable feedback and guidance that can lead to improved outcomes. The absence of mentorship hinders professional development, restricts investment in your business, and adversely affects your return on investment (ROI).

Dare to Be Different in Your Communication Strategy

Performance principles encompass four essential skills that can enhance your professional presence and effectiveness:

1. Expert Positioning: Develop your expertise and consistently showcase it. Engage in relevant training, pursue certifications, and demonstrate your skills whenever possible.

2. Signature System: Approach your speaking engagements with structure and create a transparent, repeatable process to ensure consistency and reliability in your presentations.

3. Consistent Communication: Establish a unified strategy for all your communications, including marketing and social media. This will create a strong, cohesive brand presence.

4. Mentorship: Find a mentor who can provide guidance, feedback, and support. This will accelerate your growth and enhance your professional development.

Focusing on these four essential skills can help you stand out in the competitive business landscape and achieve remarkable success.

Director Note: *Learn More Than Is Required in Your Speaking Mission*

Global Mark Keynote Speaker

Positioning yourself as a keynote speaker begins with defining your unique identity. You'll cultivate and enhance your brand, attracting clients to your business.

Last week, I was in London, and one of my favourite shops is the Apple Store. We instantly recognise the Apple Store's proposition: "Buy a Mac and don't look back." There's no need to ponder what the Apple Store represents; it embodies the iPhone, the Mac, and the exceptional experience Apple products provide. Steve Jobs was adamant that Apple products were all about the experience.

As a CEO, let me ask you: Do your products and services create an experience? If not, how can you make that happen?

Can you envision your future as a conference speaker? The world has undergone dramatic changes, and your operations must adapt accordingly. Ask yourself, "Am I an expert in my knowledge, skills, ideas, and experiences?" As a speaker, do people know about my company? Do they recognise that we are unparalleled? If not, it's time to approach things differently.

Becoming an Influential Event Speaker

To establish yourself as an outstanding speaker in the business realm, you must utilise various facets of communication. Let's explore how to achieve this and avoid common pitfalls that can undermine your credibility.

Avoiding Common Pitfalls

Have you ever wanted to crouch under the table while listening to a speaker? I recall an incident involving a well-known rugby player who dropped hundreds of pages of notes just before taking the stage. Was it amusing? Perhaps. Was it comfortable? Definitely not.

Typical speakers often rely on a vague outline and an unstructured approach, which can result in such mishaps.

Ten Characteristics of Performance Speakers

In contrast, extraordinary speakers prioritise their audience's experience and focus on what the audience truly needs to know. Here are the key characteristics and strategies that distinguish performance-based speakers:

Audience-Centred Approach

- **One:** Understand Your Audience. Identify your audience's needs and pain points, and tailor your message to address them.

- **Two:** Connect with Empathy. Show genuine understanding and care for their concerns. This fosters strong bonds and trust.

- **Three:** Organised Preparation. Develop a clear, logical structure that guides your audience effortlessly through your presentation. Each section should build on the previous one, culminating in a persuasive conclusion.

- **Four:** Practise and Refine. Rehearse your presentation multiple times. Familiarity with your material reduces reliance on notes and boosts confidence.

- **Five:** Creative Delivery. Use stories to illustrate your points. Stories are memorable and help make abstract concepts relatable.

- **Six:** Visual Aids. Utilise visuals to enhance your message. Avoid overwhelming slides filled with text; instead, use images, charts, and infographics to emphasise key points.

- **Seven:** Dynamic Body Language. Your body language should convey confidence and enthusiasm. Use deliberate gestures and movements to emphasise your points.

- **Eight:** Interactive Elements. Incorporate questions, polls, or activities that engage the audience. This keeps them involved and makes the session more dynamic.

- **Nine:** Solicit Feedback. After your presentation, seek input from trusted colleagues or mentors. Use this feedback to improve your skills further.

- **Ten:** Continuous Learning. To consistently elevate your craft, attend workshops, read books about public speaking, and observe other outstanding speakers.

Performance-based speakers view their presentations as a form of creative art. They develop and deliver a solution-oriented framework designed to enhance the audience's experience. By focusing on these strategies, you can significantly improve your communication skills and establish yourself as a powerful and influential speaker in the business world.

By embracing these practices, you will improve your speaking skills and build a reputation for delivering impactful, engaging presentations that leave a lasting impression on your audience.

Director Note: *The Best Speakers Are Continual Learners, Evolving Their Knowledge to Stay Relevant*

Speech Structuring in Various Contexts

1. Numerical Structure

Recent research and findings from *BBC News* on bowel cancer have highlighted clinicians using a step-by-step numerical framework to inform their teams about current initiatives.

2. Compare and Contrast

Businesses can use a compare-and-contrast approach to highlight their competitive advantage. As seen in *Apple vs Microsoft*, Steve Jobs often emphasised the contrast between the two companies in his presentations.

Jobs showcased remarkable expertise by drawing attention to the advanced features of Microsoft's core products. He pointed out that while Microsoft dominated the market, its delivery appeared lacklustre, whereas his own presentations sparked excitement and engagement.

3. Showcasing Formula

This method is ideal for creatively positioning and promoting your business through a challenge-and-solution framework. I use it to help clients demonstrate tangible results. Peter Drucker once said, *"As soon as you're one step from the bottom, your effectiveness depends on your ability to reach others through spoken words."*

4. Logical Chronological Structure

Health and safety presentations, which often involve logistics, legislation, and compliance, benefit from a chronological framework. This was especially evident during the COVID-19 pandemic, when infection control processes needed to be urgently tightened. Jason Leitch, Scotland's National Clinical Director, excelled in delivering daily updates using this approach. His messages were meticulously crafted and clearly communicated.

5. Modular Structure

When describing an innovative project, such as a business restructure or career transition, a modular, step-by-step structure is highly effective.

Elon Musk, co-founder of PayPal and Tesla Motors, is known for his ability to build strong human connections. He skilfully uses a modular approach, often delivering information progressively in boardroom settings over an extended timeline.

The Boardroom Backwards Melody

Delivering recommendations in the boardroom requires a structured strategy, beginning with results. I call this the *Backwards Melody of Presenting*. Mastering this approach can significantly increase the impact of your communication at an executive level.

Start with the Results

Beginning with successful outcomes is a powerful way to capture the board's attention. Highlighting key achievements first helps to frame the rest of the presentation with a sense of credibility and momentum.

Be Impactful in Your Recommendations

Share your milestones and core recommendations before diving into innovative ideas. Imagine the boardroom captivated, hanging on your every word, this is the power of leading with impact. It also establishes your authority from the outset.

Becoming an Evangelist in Your Performance

As a keynote speaker, you have the power to command any room by positioning yourself as an authority. Event organisers, company seminars, and corporate clients seek speakers who are respected subject matter experts.

Your role is to motivate and influence professionals and leaders through innovative and effective work strategies. The best speakers are those who not only have expertise but who use it to inspire their audience to go beyond the ordinary.

Employing a Combination of Methodologies

I deliver keynotes that combine sports and business performance methodologies. This integrated approach helps leaders gain a competitive advantage by applying principles from both domains. Here's a closer look:

One: Sports Performance Methodologies

- **Discipline and Practice:** Stress the importance of continual practice and discipline. Just as athletes train rigorously, business professionals must refine their skills regularly.

- **Teamwork and Leadership:** Draw parallels between sports teams and business teams, highlighting the importance of collaboration, strong leadership, and clear communication.

Two: Business Performance Methodologies

This section focuses on strategic planning and execution, using examples from successful businesses to reinforce key insights.

Three: Innovation and Creativity

Encourage your audience to embrace innovation and unconventional thinking. Many successful companies have achieved their breakthroughs through creative approaches.

Four: Interactive Elements

Engage your audience through questions, polls, or live activities that keep energy levels high and attention focused.

Five: Visual Storytelling

Use charts, graphs, images, and infographics to bring complex information to life. Visuals not only clarify ideas but also demonstrate your subject-matter expertise.

Six: Case Studies

Present compelling case studies that showcase successful outcomes and reinforce your credibility.

Seven: Testimonials

Include endorsements from satisfied clients or collaborators to boost trust and confidence in your message.

Eight: Summarise Key Points

Recap your main takeaways clearly and succinctly to reinforce the key messages of your presentation.

Nine: Actionable Steps

Provide practical, actionable steps your audience can implement immediately. Leave them with value they can apply straight away.

Stage presence can elevate your speech from a basic talk to a powerful keynote or executive-level presentation. These strategies not only enhance your performance but also solidify your reputation as a compelling speaker in the corporate world.

Director Note: *Presence, Eloquence, Grace, and Beautiful Words Are the Essence of Great Keynotes*

The Art and Craft of Stage Presence

Mastering gravitas and stage presence will make your delivery appear effortless and keep the audience engaged from start to finish.

When you walk onto the stage, begin at centre stage to deliver your opening remarks with clarity and poise. Move with intention, avoid aimless pacing, which can make you appear uncertain. Every movement should be purposeful and aligned with your message.

My background and training in film and media led me to create *Different Stages,* a performance-based methodology designed to help business professionals craft powerful presentations and sales pitches, as well as attract new clients.

This method empowers you to speak with confidence, impact, and influence, positioning you as a dynamic, performance-driven communicator.

Studying theatre and attending regular performances shifted my perspective on stagecraft. In theatre, expression is everything. Great performers use vocal variety, compelling storytelling, and emotionally engaging content to move from villain to hero, all in service of delivering a powerful, unforgettable message.

Public speaking resembles acting. It is a performance that unfolds before your eyes. Speakers, like actors, differ in their confidence and emotional stability. Master new techniques, and you will become a formidable act to follow.

Director Note: *Be a Performer, Not a Presenter*

Emotional Presence

Being a relaxed speaker is essential for delivering outstanding performances. However, relaxation should be balanced with moments of rest to maintain energy and sharp focus. To achieve this, incorporate daily mindfulness practices and establish a solid recovery plan.

What Is a Great Emotive State?

Great speakers possess emotional stability. This includes learning to use diaphragmatic breathing to calm nerves and regain composure. This type of breathing supports the vocal cords and posture, giving speakers a more powerful and commanding voice.

The Technique of Improvisation

Have you watched Ant & Dec, particularly on *I'm a Celebrity*? They excel at improvisation, effortlessly engaging audiences with unscripted humour. This skill is invaluable for speakers, enabling them to think quickly and adapt in the moment.

If you lose your way, a useful technique is to close your lips, pause, and start afresh. Mastering improvisation adds a powerful tool to your speaking repertoire.

Body Language

Great leaders demonstrate presence through an open posture and skillful use of Body Language to enhance communication and performance.

In *Beauty and the Beast*, Emma Watson's stage presence is evident through her posture, hand gestures, and body language, all reflecting confidence, elegance, and eloquence. Her open and engaging presence starkly contrasts with the grumpy, unapproachable Beast.

Open Posture and Gestures

Exceptional speakers use open posture and hand gestures to complement their stage performance. This approach enriches their presentation and helps build rapport with the audience.

Their words connect seamlessly with their gestures, creating a more engaging and effective communication style.

Focusing on relaxation, a vibrant state, improvisation, and body language can significantly enhance your speaking skills, resulting in impactful and memorable performances.

Director Note: *Gestures and Expressions Can Enhance or Undermine the Spoken Word*

The Power of Vocal Dynamics

Vocal delivery can make or break a presentation. An exceptional vocal performance captivates your audience, whereas a monotonous delivery can dull even the most exciting content. It's common to attend presentations where speakers lack clarity and struggle to engage their listeners.

Creating Enthusiasm and Energy

Your voice should generate enthusiasm and energy. It must convey emotion, humour, and, importantly, the power of a well-timed pause. Pausing before making a significant point can greatly enhance its impact.

Techniques for Effective Vocal Use

Learning to use your voice effectively is an invaluable skill. Here are some techniques to master:

One: Varying Volume

- **Soft:** Use a soft voice for delicate, emotional, or challenging topics.

- **Regular:** Speak at a normal volume for the majority of your content.

- **Loud:** Increase your volume when discussing successes or emphasising key points.

Two: Avoid Monotony

Speaking in a flat, monotonous voice can undermine your credibility. Learn techniques for varying your pitch to keep your audience engaged.

Three: Using Pitch and Tone

- **Adjust Pitch:** Modify your pitch according to the content to maintain interest.

- **Alter Tone:** Align your tone with your message, for instance, using an enthusiastic tone when discussing achievements.

Four: Pauses and Beats

Think of your voice as a finely tuned engine with multiple gears. In film and media, these shifts are known as beats and pauses. Use pauses to allow your words to resonate and build anticipation.

Director Note: *Your Voice Is the Most Powerful Tool on Stage. Vary Your Tone, Pitch, and Pace.*

Crafting Memorable Stories

Great speakers share remarkable, unforgettable stories drawn from their businesses, areas of expertise, personal lives, or even film experiences. Remember, you're weaving yourself into the narrative. People will never forget how you made them feel.

When you tell a story, you invite your audience into an experience they'll easily recall. Whether your talk aims to present data or share personal insight, you create a journey, collecting compelling moments to incorporate into future presentations for maximum effect.

Oh, and one more thing: you choose the story. Every tale features a hero and a new direction. Include an unexpected twist your audience would least expect.

I sat in the cinema for the third time in a week, reflecting on my coursework while studying Film and Media at the

University of Stirling. I remembered John, my lecturer, setting me my media assignment:

"Sheena, I want you to come back and tell me what makes a good movie. Study it from beginning to end. Share what you see and hear, looking for emotional shifts."

Help! I had my work cut out as I munched on my popcorn.

"But more importantly, I want you to examine the characters, the narrative, and the dialogue. What was it about the characters that defined the film?"

Principles of a Great Presentation

The same principles that make a great Hollywood film also create an exceptional keynote speech, executive presentation, or sales pitch. Imagine crafting a speech with extraordinary stories that inspire your colleagues and motivate your audience.

Do we really need an Oscar-winning film director to write a great speech? Probably not, but we can certainly learn from the techniques and processes directors use. Great speakers are both innovative and creative. One essential technique I teach in my masterclasses is using scenes to demonstrate a simple yet powerful method for crafting stories and building outstanding presentations.

The Power of Scenes

Audiences appreciate it when you organise your presentation or sales pitch using compelling stories structured in scenes. Recently, I skillfully used scenes one, two, and three to demonstrate a case study. This approach is highly effective in corporate settings, especially when explaining statistics, logic, or client successes. It allows you to command the room while keeping your audience captivated and engaged.

Incorporate cinematic techniques to command your space and maintain audience interest. As an exceptional storyteller, you transport your audience into your narrative with unexpected twists and emotional turns. Establish the scene before immersing your listeners, it's essential for keeping them engaged. Setting the scene and sequence of events is crucial because your audience needs to visualise the context before they can fully immerse themselves in your story.

Following these principles and incorporating storytelling techniques can enhance your presentations, keeping your audience engaged and making your message unforgettable.

Director Note: *Develop Impactful Storytelling Techniques.*

TED-Style Speaking (Technical, Entertaining, Design)

I listened with bated breath as Chris Anderson, the curator of TED, delivered training on what makes a great TED speaker. What distinguishes TED speakers from others? After all, our market is saturated with all types of speakers, some excellent, others self-proclaimed experts. So, what can we learn from TED?

Over the past decade, TED has raised the bar for presentations and speeches. Delivering a dull PowerPoint presentation is no longer sufficient. Speakers must possess charisma, humour, and a well-structured talk.

I appreciate that TED Talks give you 18 minutes to present your idea on stage. During this time, you need to convey a powerful message. When company leaders and

CEOs adopt this approach, their speaking becomes more memorable, inspiring, and likely to drive change. TED-style speaking is an excellent way to establish yourself as an authority in your field.

If you're a business professional, speaker, coach, or trainer, the essence of the TED format makes it highly relevant for your organisation. In just 18 minutes, if you're a speaker or subject-matter expert, why wouldn't you want to become that influential conversationalist?

TED Talks attract speakers and presenters from around the globe, catering to leaders, newcomers, and seasoned professionals alike. Imagine, as senior executives and CEOs, elevating your presentations and boosting your company's image, rather than simply being a dull conveyor of information. A key element of TED speeches is that each location features a specific theme.

Designing Your TEDx Talk

One: Do you have an idea worth sharing, one that delivers a memorable message and captivates your audience?

Two: Craft a journey for your audience by creating a narrative that engages both their logic and emotions as they navigate your content.

Three: You may already have a strong communication style as a speaker. TED can help you refine your strengths, build confidence, and develop a unique voice.

Four: I enjoy TED Talks because speakers do not depend on notes or cue cards. TED speakers present from memory, so it's essential to learn methods to reduce reliance on notes and shape your presentation effectively.

Five: Understand how to edit a talk so it focuses only on the critical information, removing unnecessary waffle.

Six: Great TED speakers find it easier to include memorable elements such as props, analogies, stories, and impactful phrases.

Seven: You must design, prepare, plan, and practise. This gives you time to build a bold and powerful talk.

Eight: Many speakers today present facts and information that could be far more engaging. Numerous speakers have jumped on the trauma-storytelling bandwagon. Personally, I prefer keynote speakers to trauma-focused speakers. However, the world has changed, and many people now appreciate hearing others' stories of struggle and resilience.

We discuss artificial intelligence, innovation, creativity, and thinking like a future-focused artist. This is the reality of TED Talks: you deliver something new.

Nine: Now, think about one idea, direction, or outcome you could share with your TED audience.

Let's start with the essentials of innovation and creativity for a meaningful discussion. Now is the time to clarify your ideas. Do you have a concept central to your expertise that you want to focus on?

It's time to "do or ditch" and "clear the clutter" so your audience can fully comprehend your message.

Can you share your reflections on the topic, along with others' perspectives, considering it from a futurist's viewpoint?

Director Note: *Make Time to Do a TED Talk to Position Yourself as a Quantum Leader.*

The performance is shaped not only by the words we speak, but by the presence we command. Before you take your next stage, review these Directors Notes to refine your voice and impact.

Director Note

Chapter 2: Speaking to Lead

- Your voice is your vehicle. As director, you decide the message, mood, and moment. Speak to move, not just to inform.

- Record and review a 60-second message that showcases your signature style.

- Practice pausing the silence between your words is where power lives.

- Identify your 'lane 4' stage where you perform at your highest.

- Refresh one piece of your brand voice across digital or in-person platforms.

Sheena

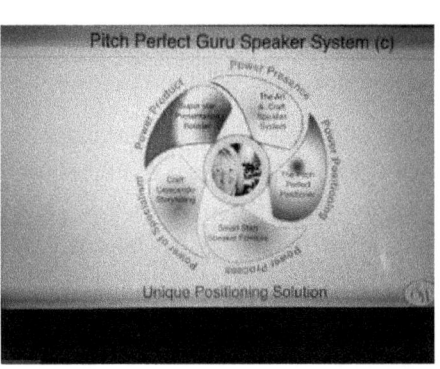

Say Yes First, Be the Best, Then Be First

Chapter 3
The Art of Infinite Coaching

"Elite coaching doesn't happen by chance it's designed, directed, and delivered with intent." Sheena Walker

"Coaching is The Art of Leading People to Achieve Their Potential."

Have you noticed that the world is changing?

We live in a dynamic economy where it is increasingly challenging to work in the field, maintain a competitive edge, and establish yourself as the go-to person or company.

Pushing performance boundaries as an executive can be a personal and professional challenge. Achieving the results that elevate you to the peak of your profession is among the primary goals of executives and business professionals. How are these results generated? What sets elite performers apart from the average individual? As a young athlete, national coach, and Special Olympics manager, I will never forget this experience, which is as relevant now as it was in the Peak Performance Pyramid of coaching and personal development.

As an athlete, my coach, Mr Blair, was clear about mental preparedness, performance, grit, and determination to be the best every day. I remember being told I had bad habits and that I'd never be successful because I kept fixing things.

Let me ask you: do you keep fixing things? You may need to learn new habits.

I listened carefully to Paul McGinley, the Ryder Cup captain, as I watched the tournament at Gleneagles. He was employing the fast-forward feedback method to assist players. You might be surprised to learn he was joined by the most unlikely performance coach, Sir Alex Ferguson. Both coach the players to execute plays that their opponents would not expect. These are two distinctly different approaches to achieving world-class coaching standards. What if you were taught to develop the grit, determination, and mental preparedness of an athlete? Would you become Olympic-ready?

Imagine having the mindset to be efficient and practical like the Ryder Cup golfers. Are you at the top of your game, or sitting on a park bench, watching others play, wishing you could join in as well?

What does it take to be a star performer? What can we emulate from performers? Every day, they have a performance director. Imagine having a director in the business world: an experienced, highly trained performance coach who provides you with the tools, tips, and techniques to develop winning business strategies.

During the lockdown, I applied my approach to help business owners challenged by severe financial implications. Sharing my methodology demands immediate correction and a new direction. Thinking like a Corporate Athlete, you can execute a play in less than 24 hours. Imagine using this framework to take your business from the pit lane to the fast track of performance. Are you committed, or will you find an excuse?

We operate in a dynamic economy where self-proclaimed experts are entering the market. It is time to step up. We need to have a competitive edge in all we do to become the go-to company and an employer of choice. Winning isn't everything; it is the only thing.

My research changed everything. After studying and learning from sports and business, I shared with my customers and clients how renewing their minds can transform them.

In this chapter, I'll share how you can become game-ready by learning the seven rules of High-Performance coaching, which serve as the magic tool for performance, productivity, and profitability.

World-Class Athletes Have World-Class Coaches

Do athletes need to push the boundaries of what has been achieved before? Adam Peaty, a world-class swimmer, competed at the Paris Olympics and, for many, the Commonwealth Games in Birmingham, as well as the Ryder Cup and the Davis Cup. Did you listen to the commentators and interviews with athletes, and notice how the word "coach" comes up repeatedly? Many credited the coaches with outstanding performances.

After winning the Ryder Cup, the Great Britain team immediately went to their performance director, Paul McGinley, and motivational coach, Alex Ferguson, to share their golden moment.

Hundreds of athletes left home and moved hundreds, if not thousands, of miles to work with the right performance coach. No athlete competing at the Olympics reached this goal alone. What they achieved was done as a team with their coach!

What if you say, "I must go where no one has gone before"? It's time to think creatively and adopt a fresh perspective. Executive coaching will allow you to examine your career, values, behaviours, and responsibilities from a new perspective.

Director Note: *How Would You Choose a World-Class Business Coach*

Coaching for Performance

One dictionary definition of a coach is a private trainer for athletes. They prepare individuals for an exam and act as specialist teachers. A coaching journey entails stopping at various destinations along the way. Leaders who coach will unlock vast reserves of human potential.

Executive Speech and Presentation Coaches

Fill this role for those serious about becoming better speakers and presenters. The coach is the individual who helps someone set and reach their goals. They take their "client" to levels they would not have attained independently. They see qualities and talents a person often doesn't know they have. Professional speech coaching helps you develop, design, and deliver brilliant presentations to become an authority in communicating an excellent business message.

Director Note: *Time to Take Your Executive Role Seriously*

A Great Coach Will Teach and Motivate!

The greatest college sports teams know the value of first-class coaching. They compete for the best coaches, who are among the highest-paid personnel at all universities. The University of Stirling has top coaches from Australia, the USA, and New Zealand. Professional athletes and athletic teams rely heavily on expert coaches. Although the team may provide one, some individuals hire their own. They believe having the right performance coach is essential to their success. Scotland's Andy Murray changed coaches four times when his performance did not match his aspirations to achieve world acclaim.

Director Note: *Pursue Excellence to Maximise Your Performance*

Authors Specialising as Editors

JK Rowling is one of the most successful and accomplished authors. She experienced a rough time before finding success, but now, she's a respected voice in literature. After hitting rock bottom, being homeless, and having no direction, she was turned down 12 times before she had a book coach.

An editor will find ways to improve writing that the author will rarely see, they're too close to it! A trained set of expert eyes will enhance the final product, from correcting spelling and grammatical errors to suggesting more effective ways to convey ideas.

The age of customisation has brought us personal trainers, personal shoppers, and personal computers. Now, we are seeing a surge in personal development services aimed at advancing your career. With an executive book coach, you will not only refine your book idea but also achieve much more. What is your vision of becoming an author?

Director Note: *Is Writing a Calling or a Compulsion?*

Coaching in Political Campaigns

Winston Churchill said, "If you are going through hell, keep going."

I guarantee that many political candidates will be coached in their communication skills. Some individuals slipped in their speech during the primary elections and are no longer in the running.

Although there may be other reasons for their withdrawal, a poorly debated performance never helped a politician. Political debates can make or break a political career.

Great script coaching is one way to ensure they do their best. Observe Rishi Sunak, Liz Truss, and other candidates vying for the position of Prime Minister through public speaking and panel debates. Recent BBC debates were embarrassing, as they frequently interrupted each other and held conflicting views on critical topics. I understand that politicians received feedback during this leadership campaign. An appalling, detrimental comment on a BBC debate by Liz Truss, "I'm not too good at presentation." How unbelievable. Was she going through hell?

As politicians or civil servants, we are in a profession that requires us to speak publicly. The key to success is not to push your speeches, but to demonstrate and be an expert in your subject.

Director Note: *Learn How to Design, Develop, and Deliver Powerful Presentations*

Where Speakers Become World-Class Communicators

Have you been part of a speaker group? Consider the evaluation and feedback of their regular business meetings. The most crucial part of feedback is a mini coaching session.

Like a professional coach, a good evaluator will complement the speaker on aspects of their presentation, identify an area that needs improvement, and finish with another compliment. Have you ever thought about the similarities between work, speaking, and sport? That was a remarkable moment. How often can you go into that meeting, presentation, or interview without proper training or preparation? So, whether you are training for your next triathlon or getting ready for an important work event, be mindful of all the different factors involved and prepare for each accordingly.

Will you inspire your team? Your new coaching skills focus on helping you achieve your personal bests. We adhere to a simple philosophy: do things correctly. No excuses. No exceptions. While not everyone may be an athlete, we find great satisfaction in a job well done, transforming you from Mr Average in business to something truly extraordinary. How can we lead the field in a saturated market filled with self-proclaimed experts?

Director Note: *Elevate Your Influence Speaking Engagements in Professional Spaces*

Are You the Masterpiece or a Self-Proclaimed Expert?

What comes to mind when you hear the word "masterpiece"? A work of art, recognised worldwide as a brilliant creation by an artist, architect, sculptor, or any creative individual who has left their mark on society. You would be correct. Let's briefly consider whether you and I could become the centrepiece that achieves this. Could we be that masterpiece?

Let's take a moment to reflect on Michelangelo, Rembrandt, Pablo Picasso, Vincent van Gogh, and Leonardo da Vinci. What do they all have in common?

Leonardo da Vinci spent four challenging years painting the *Mona Lisa*, going around in circles with shapes and colours, uncertain of his progress. Why? He needed the guidance of a skilled mentor. Expecting it to be a masterpiece without corrections or clear direction would be unheard of in world-class sport. Would you agree? Are you a Leonardo da Vinci who is four years older and still stuck?

There are an easier way and a great starting point for self-mastery. The time is now to move from ordinary to making decisions with clear intentions, learning from the best, 5, 4, 3, 2, 1. It is time to execute the play so no one will anticipate your next move.

Director Note: *Reflect on Levels 1–10 Where Do You Stand in Your Performance?*

Time to Pause, Reset, and Re-engineer Your System

Every company and manager aim to help their employees maximise their potential. Traditional management styles have limitations; however, research shows that Peak Performance coaching improves productivity and staff performance.

Understanding how to assist others in achieving their peak performance is one of the most valuable skills for any leader or business professional. The key lies in generating increased revenue, acquiring skills to become a high-performance coach, and observing staff enhance performance and productivity. The methods and strategies employed in high-performance coaching draw extensively from sport and the military, where optimal performance is essential. High-performance coaching discussions typically begin by identifying individuals' "starting points", their visions, or life goals.

Next, it examines individuals' paths and actions to realise those visions. Ordinary people adapt to the world, while extraordinary individuals shape their own.

Director Note: *Which World Are You Planning to Make the Centrepiece Professionally?*

7 Steps in the Art of Self-Mastery Results

You don't need to be an extraordinary hero to take steps towards competition. You can be average and motivated enough to achieve challenging goals. Setting intentions is one of the most effective training tools available. Goals help organise competitors' focus and efforts towards accomplishing specific tasks. They also enhance persistence and motivation for long-term training. Having a clear intention can help a performer discover new learning strategies. Unfortunately, people's goals are often set incorrectly. If you wish to establish or reassess new goals, follow these seven steps for practical goal-setting:

One: Define Your Intentions

Consider these critical questions:

What do you want to achieve?

What accomplishment would be deserving of your utmost effort?

What would you try if you knew it was impossible to fail?

What would you do if you knew this was your final opportunity?

Ensure your vision is clear and powerful, and persevere in pursuing it despite setbacks or failures. The goal should be specific (e.g., "My goal is to be placed in the top ten of my industry") rather than vague or general, allowing you to assess whether you have achieved it.

Two: Where Are You Right Now?

Carefully assess your current situation in relation to your goal. Have you been getting by, or are you preparing to reach the next level? Are you ready to take actions you might not prefer, in order to accomplish your goal? Recognise when you feel at your best and what fosters that environment. Don't just blend in, create your world.

Three: Be Honest About What You Need to Lead You

To reach your destination, you must understand how to get there. How will you advance with new methods and structures? In what types of situations do you excel or falter? Identify at least one area in each of the following skill categories that requires improvement:

Physical (e.g., increases in speed)

Tactical (e.g., developing a winning strategy)

Technical (e.g., more precise point control)

Mental (e.g., greater confidence)

Four: Formulate a Daily Improvement Plan

This is the most crucial step in the goal-setting process. Ask yourself, "What can I do daily to reach my goal?" For each area identified in step 3, write at least three or four specific actions you can take. Phrase them as "I" statements and in the present tense. For example, if you need to improve your speed, you might write, "I do my exercises for fifteen minutes three times a week." You are more likely to follow that than the statement, "I will get faster legs."

Five: Make and Work on Short-Term Goals

High performance, as outlined in step 1, may require a considerable amount of time, ranging from months to even years. Set short-term goals to keep yourself motivated during this period. Achieving these goals will provide feedback on your progress towards your ultimate aim. These goals should be process-oriented and reflect that reaching your goal is an ongoing journey.

Each day, I ask myself important questions that start with the letter P:

How did I perform yesterday?

Could I do better?

Am I positioning myself?

Do I have a presence in my market?

Am I demonstrating strength in my service delivery?

Can you see the power of transition here?

Six: You Must Commit to Learning from the Best

It's easy to say you'll do something; doing it is another story. This is analogous to people who make New Year's resolutions to be different, yet seldom follow through. Second-guessing yourself, missing opportunities, and hesitating will only delay your eventual success. Keep reminding yourself to enjoy the journey along the way!

I am studying Leadership at the Sandhurst Military Academy. Can you imagine a soldier saying, "I won't follow the rules today"? No, they have to upgrade their internal systems constantly.

Seven: Observe Your Process

Every day, ask yourself, "Am I getting closer to my goal?" Is your goal plan working, or does it need adjustment? If your answer is, "I'm not sure," then you are not progressing. Write down your small successes and lessons learned, or create a checklist that charts your progress. In times when it seems like your goal is too far out of reach, you can look at your progress list and visually see how far you've come, and how much closer you are to achieving your goal.

My Gram and Groom model enhances your self-mastery skills, enabling you to achieve outstanding results.

Director Note: *Are You Caged, Comfortable, or Charged with Action?*

The Gram & Groom Results Method ©

- **G**: Great Positioning
- **R**: Result Sales
- **A**: An Aspirational Leader
- **M**: Motivational Intelligence Critical Success Factors
- **G**: Great Coaching
- **Reality**: Where are you?
- **O**: Opportunity New Direction
- **Obstacles**: Remove the Boulder
- **M**: Motivational Action

Say Yes

Coaching is an intentional craft and the best directors never leave growth to chance. These notes are your prompts to lead with clarity, care, and command.

Director Note

Chapter 3: Coaching by Design

- Coaching is not correction its direction with distinction. Be the coach who edits for excellence and inspires legacy-level results.

- Define your coaching stance in 10 words or less.

- Design a 3-step result ritual for every client session.

- Ask one bold question that unlocks change.

- Audit your client journey is every scene necessary?

Say Yes to World Class Branding for Success

Chapter 4
Laser Leadership Archetypes

"True leaders don't follow scripts they write them. Every move is a message." Sheena Walker

"You Are Not Being Judged, The Value of What You Bring to the Audience Is." Seth Godin

In today's dynamic economy, the calibre and quality of leadership provided by senior executives and CEOs are critical for success in both industry and commerce.

In laser leadership, we expect leaders to serve as ambassadors with a clear vision and direction. They should understand exactly what to do and grasp the key success factors of action-oriented leadership.

We assume they can lead a team, manage people's expectations, and drive a regional, national, or global business. Great leaders have meaningful conversations, radiate energy, and exhibit influential power in boardrooms and team meetings. They can command any stage in any environment.

Leaders with class maintain a strong emotional state when facing challenges such as disasters, recessions, and economic disruptions. They are leaders of change who must be proactive in managing change.

Why do we need more leadership skills and people-centred leaders who don't believe they require training? They understand that an organisation cannot simply remain static; it either grows or declines. Why do leaders lack the courage and ability to guide their organisations through the challenges, difficulties, and changes in our economy? The answer is simple, they lack the essential skills to lead their people, and this can have serious consequences.

Great companies are led by great leaders. Think of people like Amazon's Jeff Bezos and the late Steve Jobs, who prioritised leadership and simplicity in developing systems and processes, which helped position their brands and people for success.

I attended a postgraduate leadership course at the University of Stirling, delivered by the renowned Sandhurst Military Academy. Initially, I viewed this leadership approach as different from my own, but I quickly realised that decisive, direct leadership was necessary. I was fascinated to learn that entry-level cadets were being trained in leadership from a real-world perspective.

Military leadership is akin to leading athletes, requiring confidence, self-belief, assertiveness, and decision-making. The power of action leadership, decision-making, problem-solving, and motivation, was clearly evident.

Could you build a leadership empire in the business world and create a high-performing culture? Imagine if you had a methodology that positions you as the go-to person in your organisation and earns you the title of "Ambassadorial Leader."

Becoming a different-stage leader means developing your unique style and shifting your thinking towards results, influential conversations, and powerful boardroom interactions. Breaking the rules of conventional leadership and transforming them into a working model of laser leadership can help you create a motivated team and inspire extraordinary results.

In this chapter, I will share the nine laws of situational leadership that will shape your future and help you become a laser-focused leader. You will learn how leadership styles can be situational and context-dependent, and how to develop your skills, energy, and direction.

Dare to Embrace a Different Approach

Our dynamic economy has forced us to reconsider emergency services, which has led to unintentional leadership.

Think of leadership as a diverse range of skills, such as creating new ways to make decisions and mastering your time. Your ability to improve performance and effectiveness as a leader depends on your capacity to influence and be influenced by your team, develop individual talent, and build a team that speaks the talk, walks the talk, and takes action.

Law One: The Winning Difference of a Scientific Laser Leader

Truly great leaders understand that they are part of a team, looking outward from within. How do you define success in the pursuit of excellence? We are tackling the challenges of a demanding business environment and a saturated market, striving to lead the field. Our competitive advantages stem from our ability to learn quickly and adapt to change. Imagine if you had winning performance strategies at your team's disposal, similar to those of an Olympic athlete. Can you envision the results?

Great managers understand their people and recognise that excellent performance relies on both their management style and the employees' efforts. Effective managers grasp their employees' skills, concerns, needs, and levels of motivation. They understand that if they neglect these diverse needs, employees are more likely to waste energy moving in the wrong direction, feel frustrated by a lack of progress, or disengage from the team or project. Have you encountered this?

Knowing how to help others achieve their highest performance is the most valuable skill any leader or businessperson can possess. It's also the secret to improving staff morale and motivation. A leader who is heart-centred promotes teamwork and loyalty, inspiring people to work together, while instilling confidence and passion in those they lead.

Achieving results that elevate you to the top of your game is a key goal for any business professional. How are these results created? What sets elite performers apart from the average person? The answer lies in ambassadorial leadership.

To achieve excellence, it is essential to cultivate daily personal and professional habits. By developing expertise and self-discipline, you can make informed decisions that yield exceptional results. Implementing a strategy focused on critical success factors will help you meet and exceed high-performance standards.

Coaching staff to maximise productivity and performance is essential for gaining a competitive edge, establishing quality standards and best practices is crucial for effective change management. By imparting diverse skills, actions, and behaviours, you foster mental preparedness, positioning yourself as a unique leader and making you and your company the go-to resource in your field.

As an executive, dedicating yourself to learning and continually enhancing your leadership skills is essential for achieving exceptional results. Imagine spending 60 minutes daily as a student of leadership, refining your craft and committing to a lifelong learning approach. The greatest athletes often possessed less innate skill than their competitors, yet their remarkable dedication, commitment, and drive to maximise their strengths made them iconic. Now is the time to leverage situational leadership to elevate performance in your organisation, embracing the mental preparedness and unwavering dedication of an athlete.

Director Note: *Definitive Leadership by Design. Train Your People Scientifically.*

Law Two: Who is to Blame? Who Makes Decisions?

Returning from another trip to Australia, I eagerly shared with my family everything I had seen, the people I had met, and the insights I had gained into their education and social systems. I was taken aback when my younger son said, "Mum, we're not interested in Australia. We have no intention of going there. We are Scottish, enjoying Scotland, the hills, and all that comes with it. Why don't you get back to sharing your business world with us? That's far more interesting."

This comment halted the conversation, highlighting how deeply ingrained people's habits can be. Are you also operating on autopilot in your professional life? Is there a need for transformation? Can individuals genuinely change their ways of thinking?

Sheena L.C. Walker

Reflecting as a futurist, I pondered not the past or the present, but on what the future holds for us, both personally and professionally. Why do our mindsets often confine us?

Standing in what appeared to be an Amazon warehouse brimming with packages and boxes, I reflected on my son's resolute choice to remain in Scotland. Yet here I was, witnessing his new journey: moving from the Scottish islands to Australia. Despite months of organising, planning, and international correspondence, I struggled to grasp how he would reach his destination. Is your business equally chaotic, like a jigsaw puzzle with missing pieces?

My house was jam-packed, the garden complete, the garage cluttered with boxes, and the lounge unrecognisable. As the countdown to his flight began, 40 hours, then 24, I wondered how we would organise all his belongings. Amidst the chaos, my son asked for two new white shirts and a pair of shoes from Marks & Spencer. This added layer of complexity made me question my decision-making under pressure. Have you ever had to make swift decisions or drastically change direction in your professional life? Was it chaotic?

Surprisingly, my son chose to travel lightly, taking only the essentials and leaving behind any excess baggage. This minimalist approach starkly contrasts with the overloaded, indecisive leadership style often observed in business. Have you ever felt so overwhelmed that you opted to walk away, starting anew with minimal baggage in a different country?

What does this new direction, this fresh start, signify? It reminds us that sometimes embracing both excess and simplicity can lead to a more rewarding and professional path.

Was there an overhaul ahead? Can people truly change their thinking and how they operate? Reflecting as a futurist, I considered not the past or the present, but the future and what it holds for us, both personally and professionally. Why are we so often caged by our mindsets?

About six hours after the plane departed for Australia, I drove home to what felt like an Amazon warehouse filled with my son's boxes, clothes, motorbikes, and everything he owned. Where would I even begin? Let's reflect on what just happened. My previous trips and conversations had been rather dull.

This situation represented a strange leap into Leadership Mastery. Neil didn't use the term "design thinking," but I believe he was innovative and creative, considering the future in a different light. Was he acting as a futurist, stepping into the unknown? He embraced the notion that life could be vastly different in Australia without mentioning resources or planning skills.

The dynamic changes in our economy over the past two years have forced individuals and organisations to rethink their operations. Many remain on pause, hoping that sticking to old habits will yield results. However, leaders with mastery take the seemingly impossible and make it happen.

In sharp contrast to Neil's thinking, Jeff Bezos of Amazon applied design thinking to their services just three weeks into the pandemic. Recognising a significant opportunity in online food shopping and other commodities, he took a risk and committed fully to inspiring others with his ambitious vision.

Bezos exhibited leadership at the highest level, making significant decisions and being confident enough to take risks that promised substantial returns on investment. Bezos wasted no time taking action, organising his staff around a customer-centred approach and laser-focused thinking. He pushed the limits of performance, a key priority for Amazon, to maintain results and introduce new online services. Did he take leadership risks by making swift decisions? Absolutely!

What distinguishes leaders from the average person? As an influential leader, your ability to tackle difficult situations and respond to economic demands requires maintaining a state of psychological readiness. How can you achieve success beyond your current field? It centres on embracing change, taking calculated risks, and leading with vision and determination.

Being a leader of change means commanding attention in any situation. You, too, can do this when someone like Jeff Bezos shines brightly and acts decisively. Everyone has their fortune, much like a sculptor who transforms raw materials into a masterpiece. That's mastery, a skill developed and refined through dedication. To emulate Jeff Bezos, one must follow the golden rule of timing, perseverance, and persistence to achieve success.

Director Note: *Time to Become a Commercially Incomparable Leader*

Law Three: Dynamics of Design Thinking

Are you leading with a giant pause button stuck in the lift? Recently, I've spoken to individuals and companies whose buttons are genuinely stuck. My role is to help you realise that the impossible is possible. What if you incorporated design thinking into your leadership style?

Design thinking places the customer at the heart of problem-solving and innovation. This approach focuses on researching what people want from your organisation, product, or service, then developing and testing new models to deliver that experience.

So, what's different about design thinking? Traditionally, organisations reflect on existing services to find ways to make them more appealing to staff and customers. In contrast, design thinking involves generating new ideas based on how customers might use the product or service, actively listening to their wants and needs. Importantly, these ideas must also be commercially viable for you, personally or professionally.

By embracing design thinking, just as athletes strategically structure their training to achieve victory, you can break free from stagnation and steer your organisation towards innovative success. Embrace the core principles of timing, perseverance, and persistence, as Jeff Bezos did. Each individual holds their fortune, and you can shape your journey to mastery through design thinking.

Director Note: *Apply the Laws of Design Thinking to Achieve Uniqueness.*

Law Four: The Design Thinking Leader

What comes to mind when you hear the word "masterpiece"? Perhaps it evokes thoughts of a work of art, global recognition, or an exceptional artist. It denotes someone who is creative and has made a lasting impact on the world. When I first saw the Eiffel Tower, I reflected on the architectural expertise of French engineer Stephen Sauvestre. His design-oriented approach led to the Eiffel Tower being built in just two years and two months, a remarkable feat. What do leaders like Sauvestre do that distinguishes them? How can we become a central feature in our respective fields?

Think of great artists like Michelangelo, Pablo Picasso, and Leonardo da Vinci. What do they have in common? They all created masterpieces and became leaders in their respective fields. Leonardo da Vinci spent four years working on the Mona Lisa, comparing the process to piecing together a fragmented jigsaw puzzle. He lacked expert guidance and formal qualifications, often feeling as though he was stuck with the pause button on, much like many executives today. What he needed was specialised correction, direction, and mentorship. Can you relate to this? Do you hope that everything will turn out well in your business?

In our dynamic economy, futurist thinking and timely action are critical. Design thinking leadership is an individual-centred approach that prioritises customer needs and desires over innovation. If the world is changing and creativity is no longer the preserve of a few, why aren't you using design thinking more?

Design thinking transcends creative industries. It involves listening to customers, understanding their needs, and developing new ideas that are both innovative and commercially viable. Embracing this approach enables individuals to transform ideas into reality, just as artists craft raw materials into masterpieces.

These laws summarise the key qualities and actions necessary to become a Design Thinking Leader.

- **Embrace Creativity**: Move beyond conventional thinking to explore innovative solutions. Encourage yourself and your team to think creatively and openly welcome unconventional ideas.

- **Focus on the User**: Understand your customers' needs, desires, and pain points. Design solutions that effectively address these needs. By placing the user at the centre of your problem-solving process, you ensure that your solutions are relevant and impactful.

- **Iterate and Test**: Adopt an iterative approach to problem-solving. Create prototypes of your ideas and evaluate them with users to collect feedback. Use this feedback to continually refine and enhance your solutions.

- **Seek Mentorship**: Surround yourself with mentors who can offer guidance, support, and insights based on their experience. Mentors can provide valuable feedback, help you navigate challenges, and accelerate your growth as a design-thinking leader.

- **Be Persistent**: Success rarely comes without challenges and setbacks. Stay resilient and determined in the face of obstacles. Great leaders persevere through difficulties, learn from failures, and keep pushing forward toward their goals.

By embodying these principles and practising them in your leadership approach, you can become a more effective design-thinking leader who drives innovation and delivers impactful solutions.

Director Note: *Adjust your leadership perspective to teach others new skills, create exceptional work, and emphasise craftsmanship. There's only one version of you. Go forth and embody that masterpiece.*

Law Five: To Lead a Giant Life Starts with Giant-Class Thinking

First-class leadership is about having a clear vision and effectively communicating it to both the market and the public. Great leaders do not solely focus on success nor fear the extent of their influence. They prioritise the essentials of innovation and sometimes protect their ideas. When I mention companies like Apple, BMW, Ferrari, Ryanair, and British Airways, embodying first-class thinking requires taking actions that the remaining 99% do not pursue. Which class do they operate in? You can quickly tell me which class you're in right now. Athletes may start in economy class, but they do not stay there for long before moving to first class. How quickly will you rise to first class?

Understanding economy-class thinking means grasping the fundamentals of your industry. However, for many, this can be limiting, as they struggle to understand the basics of business.

You may find yourself in business class, feeling that you have gained knowledge, skills, and experience, yet still unsure of how to formulate a strategy that suits you. Like many others, I have observed how you flit from project to project, training, and everything else you can grab. "Brain clutter sets in as you wonder, 'What on earth do I do with all this?'" It's akin to a lengthy grocery list!

What if you nurtured exceptional thinking? What does that involve? It's about setting a high standard in every aspect of business. A model of best practices, perhaps? Now you're wondering where to start. Do you need justification for changing your business approach to stand out? We encounter average, excellent, and remarkable individuals, with some truly extraordinary people standing out. Today, I reflect differently, questioning whether my actions are merely ordinary. It's time to embrace the extraordinary. Is this commercially viable? Can you envision it?

Director Note: *First-Class Leaders, Action Giant-Class Dividends*

Law Six: Do Ambassadorial Leaders Achieve Extraordinary Performance?

My challenge is identifying the service that will deliver excellent results, enabling you to join the top 1%, change your direction, or remain average. Where do you stand? Are you comfortable or uncomfortable? You must believe in yourself and take responsibility for your personal goals, qualities, and character. Are you a caged, relaxed, or charged leader? It is time to step up to the 1% class of excellence.

Step up and embrace the challenge of personal development and leadership excellence! Strive for greatness, break free from your comfort zone, and aim to join the top 1% of performers. Believe in yourself, take responsibility for your goals, and practise relentlessly, like world-class cyclist Sir Chris Hoy.

Align with your "Zone of Genius" by harnessing your talents, skills, and character to reach peak performance. Now is the ideal moment to become an exceptional leader, presenting a higher vision, greater value, and unmatched productivity. Rise to the challenge and join the ranks of excellence today! This phrase, first encountered by Dr Gay Hendricks, author of *The Big Leap*, asserts that when you harmonise your talents, skills, and character, you truly enter your genius zone.

Director Note: *Working in Your Zone of Genius Demonstrates Willpower, Talent, and Significance*

Law Seven: Do Leaders Risk More Than Is Required?

Have you noticed that many leaders lack emotional intelligence? Today, many are arrogant, assertive, overbearing, self-important, and eager to do anything for more money. We saw this during the energy crisis. "I am powerful. They don't need it, but believe they deserve it." This reflects their perception of power status.

Why are leaders struggling with performance excellence? The world has evolved, and so must you. We now live in a very different environment compared to ten years ago. This marks the beginning of a new chapter in business performance. Your best ideas from five years ago are now outdated. Have you noticed the rapid growth of social media, online shopping, technological innovations, a global recession, and a significant shift in consumer behaviour?

Relying on outdated performance methods is no longer advisable. The traditional career escalator is stalled, and companies are now facing an unexpected reality. The impact has been felt across all markets, leading to disaster, disruption to family life, insolvency, business failures, and significant unemployment.

How can you sharpen your entrepreneurial skills, kickstart a new career, and adopt a new way of thinking to position yourself as a Corporate Athlete? Now is the time to become an exceptional leader, demonstrating a higher vision, better values, and unmatched productivity. Step up and join the ranks of excellence today.

Director Note: *Establish Real Class as the Standard for Real Results*

Law Eight: Military Leadership The Burden of Command

The military refers to this as the "burden of command." An army commander is entirely responsible for the mission and the team at all times, including the actions of team members outside of work. Successful commanders place the mission and the team above themselves.

Sometimes, the mission must take precedence over the team, which may require the commander to make unpopular or even life-or-death decisions. The cost of command is steep, and maintaining it over the long term can be exhausting. This is why the military restricts the duration of command assignments and typically reassesses commanders for roles of lesser responsibility, allowing them time to recharge before resuming command.

How can we implement a military-style leadership approach in business? This approach is straightforward and elicits an immediate response. Much like in the military, clinical governance legislation, safety regulations, and compliance with emergency planning are critical to patient care.

Military-style leadership and emergency services: Do they differ or are they similar? Both rely on an immediate chain of command that requires swift action. Emergency response teams react to 999 emergencies, managing the unexpected. They employ a leadership system known as "Triage," which categorises emergencies as A, B, or C, enabling the ambulance service to determine the best course of action in potentially life-threatening situations.

Do you operate a business without a triage system? What do you do in an emergency? How do you respond to situations proactively or reactively?

I interact daily with executives and business professionals seeking clarification on how to address business challenges. Are you in the emergency services department, managing every 999 calls? Do you have a triage system to handle situations and prioritise daily tasks?

How do your company's priorities, planning, and preparation address emergencies?

You may have considered an MBA to learn the critical success factors in business operations, HR, marketing, interpretation of financial data, social media, and performance management skills. I regularly converse with individuals who find themselves in business emergencies. They come to me seeking new ideas and directions to enhance their services.

Director Note: *Are You the Decision Maker for Red, Amber, or Green in Operating a 999 Service?*

Law Nine: The Methodical Leader in The Boardroom

Are you aware? It's no secret that the higher you climb the corporate ladder, the more crucial your leadership and public speaking skills become. Are you a futurist? Do you aspire to greater responsibilities, along with the accompanying position and salary? If so, you will need to position yourself effectively. At each stage of your career, you must market yourself, your value, your ideas, and your ability to obtain a promotion. This requires acquiring influential and impactful skills and maintaining a keen focus to guide your prospects towards a positive outcome, thereby securing that agreement or new contract.

What is the key to selling yourself and your ideas to senior management? How is it different? We understand the high stakes when communicating with stakeholders and joint ventures.

Your audience will either accept or reject the recommendations you have worked so hard on. If you are the financial or commercial director with a prominent role in your company and have been asked to submit a proposal, possibly for a contract or a new build, merely presenting facts and figures will not suffice.

In our dynamic economy, many executives I speak to face challenges, are hesitant, and struggle to deliver high-level reports and recommendations. They are realising that this gap in knowledge and skills is detrimental to the business.

I refer to this as the backwards melody of boardroom presentations, beginning in reverse. You must be clear about the subject you are presenting, and it is essential to consider some of the challenges and questions that your audience may have.

Being invited to present at a recruitment and selection assessment day offers a fantastic opportunity to showcase your potential contributions to the company. What could go wrong?

A recent conversation with a business executive revealed that the panel interrupted him five times during his presentation. This may have been partly due to rudeness, but also because his presentation lacked focus, which left the audience unclear about the topic.

This resulted in a troubled board member leaving the room. Can you mesmerise your audience in the boardroom with your Backwards Melody approach recommendations for your project? It's time to secure a resounding YES.

Say Yes

Director Note: *As an Executive, Begin with a Captivating Headline and Compelling Content to Engage Your Audience*

Leadership is the ultimate production role part visionary, part strategist. Use these final cues to direct with presence, poise, and precision.

Director Note

Chapter 4: Leadership Logistics

- Leadership isn't loud it's lived. Directors don't chase applause; they build high-performance culture, scene by scene.

- Choose one leadership moment today to elevate with intention.

- Set a clear boundary that protects your performance energy.

- Replace a routine with a ritual.

- Send one message of direction not motivation to your team.

Sheena

———

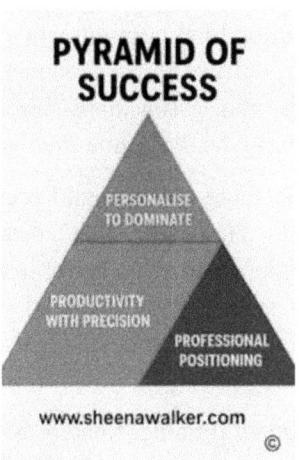

Say Yes to Elite Authority as a Leader

Chapter 5
The Training Edge Creator

"Training isn't teaching it's transforming. A master trainer rehearses results, not routines." Sheena Walker

The *Training Edge Creator* refers to a person, programme, or entity that designs and implements training programmes to give individuals or organisations a competitive advantage. This concept emphasises the significance of continuous learning and development in maintaining an edge within a rapidly changing sporting, business, or professional environment.

As a young athlete, I learned various training skills. One crucial skill was using mental rehearsal and imagery to build my confidence. This confidence stems from the understanding that physical and psychological preparation requires total commitment to training. As a young swimmer, daily training sessions, which included warm-ups, drills, and lesson plans, were integral to my routine, particularly the discipline involved.

I recognised that these skills would prepare me for the business world. However, that determination and commitment to being an elite performer was doing not develop. That regular tap on the head with a clipboard reminded me of the importance of consistently achieving my best performance.

Through exceptional training, I had to become a learning machine. When my coach yelled, "You did well today, Sheena!" I knew it was another day of performance excellence.

A champion always prepares to win, whether they are a world-class athlete, a musician, a High Court judge, a business executive, or someone working in the clinical or scientific fields.

What is it they have in common? What are the similarities? What are their differences?

What if you had a training mindset with daily accomplishments, personally and professionally?

We expect leading companies to excel in our dynamic economy. Precisely, C-suite professionals must possess the skills to influence their teams effectively. We expect corporate professionals to exemplify and have the critical success factors necessary to become the leading company. Is there an assumption that holding a title exempts one from training, or that proficiency in one role guarantees a promotion?

Executive positions are often excluded from Continuous Professional Development (CPD) or from receiving training. Have you encountered this?

Recently, while collaborating with a director with limited business understanding, it became evident that his lack of training affected his performance in a commercial setting. In the NHS, promotions are often based on years of service; no one can be promoted to a clinical lead position without adequate management training. Reflective thoughts: does insufficient training lead to a decline in standards?

I was criticised for having high standards: "We don't work like that, Sheena." My training and sports performance background prepared me well for the professional world. It showcased a high level of expertise and mastery, allowing me to lead the field and maintain a competitive edge over others.

While training with the Scottish Ambulance Service, teaching others CPR and how to save lives on community calls, what if I dropped the baton? If that were to happen, my quality standards could become life-threatening. We see this today in our dynamic economy. Is it the dropping of the baton?

Demonstrating expertise and mastery in training provides a competitive edge over others in the field. Why do athletes and business professionals experience performance–choking, anxiety, and nervousness when everything seems to be going well? Choking occurs in the competitive arena when a person fears failure in sports; the same can happen in business.

Training performance in our current economy can be affected by anxiety and nervousness, lack of confidence and preparation, and limiting beliefs that all senior executives face today.

Being an elite performer includes ensuring quality recovery time by focusing on all aspects of well-being: relaxation, recharging, and renewing daily energy. Maintaining composure under pressure is a top priority for business professionals every day.

In this chapter, I will share Ten esteemed training skills, knowledge, and experiences that can yield world-class results, akin to those of top athletes. A performance trainer teaches athletes tips and techniques that their competitors will not foresee. You could implement strategies to achieve expert positioning in the business world.

Sheena L.C. Walker

Director Note: *Champions Develop World-Class Beliefs Before They Become Champions*

Law One: Self-Master the Art of Training

A new type of celebrity has emerged: the CEO, business executives, and professional speakers who effectively convey messages that inspire change. Personal development is the foundation for self-mastery and interaction, combining two delivery styles to influence ideas, appreciate the power of persuasion, and create training programmes.

When I studied film and media at the University of Stirling, I was fascinated by how movies were constructed and how TV programmes were scheduled to enhance actors' brand image. I realised that if we applied these principles in the business world, we too could become slightly famous, as a character, a hero, or perhaps even a villain. They were being positioned so that people would talk about you, what you did, your actions, and your experience. Imagine if that occurred to you in your business as a CEO. So why doesn't it happen?

Why are C-suite and business executives reluctant to fill the training gap that would see their business triple, a gap that would give them authority, a gap that would give them a competitive edge? Perhaps, just like a character in a film, your business could be a total blockbuster, imagine a blockbuster sales academy.

Is training different from coaching and speaking? Yes, it entails a distinct set of skills. Training has been my passion for the past thirty years. It enables you to explore a concept, share it, develop it, assist others in learning it, apply it, and then utilise it to enhance your performance.

Cultivating trainers within your organisation is vital in today's economy, as it identifies individuals dedicated to learning and adaptable to change.

Director Note: *Ensure Your Training Runs Smoothly to Provide Staff with a Slightly Famous Edge*

Law Two: What is Thinking in Design Training?

What is design thinking? It involves applying knowledge to a specific skill area in business or your career, and everyone who can perform a skill has the potential to train others. When I worked for Boots, we had a super-induction programme with precise training for new starts, which developed staff both personally and professionally in the Boots design thinking style.

I train design-thinking trainers and executives in what I consider the most profitable skill in today's business world. I teach clients design mastery skills so they can deliver in an actual class.

We offer action-based, accelerated, and virtual learning in training, alongside media learning.

Become a student of design to reach your full potential by sharing your ideas, concepts, and strategies with the world.

Imagine if training and continuous learning became an intrinsic part of your DNA. Adopting this mindset could cultivate a vast reservoir of knowledge, significantly enhancing your value in the marketplace. Consider this: every concept or skill you share with your audience should first be something you have thoroughly experienced and mastered yourself.

This approach invariably yields richer, more intricate, and significantly more valuable outcomes.

You lay the groundwork to lead others effectively by committing to self-influence and self-mastery. By concentrating on personal growth, you improve your abilities, increasing your capacity to teach and inspire those around you. This continuous journey of learning and personal development transforms you into a more dynamic and influential leader in your field.

Director Note: *Champions Always Strive for First-Class Competence*

Law Three: Adopt Training Design Skills

The skill component of training is the topic you will explore and practise. It constitutes your résumé, your skill set, and your achievements. One myth about training is that individuals either believe they do not need it or do not attempt to engage with it. Although it was not a focus in their formal education, it has become essential in business.

You might be the best CEO, doctor, dentist, car mechanic, plumber, or joiner, but you may need to enhance your training skills. You could be an excellent accountant, but your approach can be repetitive and dull. You might work well, being fit or a dance school choreographer, yet people often attend just one session because you lack the necessary training skills. Training is a design methodology, a highly professional skill that leads to significant motivation.

Directors Note: *Prepare Like a World-Class Professional, Unlocking Your Next Level of Development Today*

Law Four: Training Versus Teaching

Famous football players often move straight into coaching when they retire. They possess a unique skill set and can pass it on to younger team members.

As a business executive, you may require more motivation, which can lead to low enthusiasm, inadequate skills, and a poor return on investment (ROI) for your company.

When your skills are exceptional, you will be sought after for sharing your knowledge with others.

Key Differences Between Training and Teaching

One: Objective

Training: Aimed at developing specific skills for immediate application.

Teaching: To offer a comprehensive knowledge foundation and foster critical thinking skills.

Two: Methodology

Training: More practical, experiential, and focused on tasks.

Teaching: More theoretical, comprehensive, and focused on knowledge.

Three: Outcome

Training: Mastery of a specific skill or competency.

Teaching: A comprehensive understanding of a subject area.

Overlap and Integration

Training in Education: Certain educational programmes, such as vocational schools, integrate training within a teaching framework.

Teaching in Training: Effective training programmes often incorporate teaching elements to clarify the principles behind learning tasks.

In essence, training involves acquiring specific skills for immediate application, whereas teaching entails gaining a broader understanding and developing the ability to think critically about a subject.

Both are essential in various contexts and frequently complement each other in professional and educational environments.

Director Note: *Players Are Obsessed with Results and Productivity*

Law Five: Design Trainers Are Influential Specialists

Could you be a master of influence, possessing the ability to inspire others? Imagine having the perfect blend of being a trainer and the best CEO. You can be an educator, CEO, businessperson, or entrepreneur. The moment you stand before a group, you are there for them.

Trainers hold tremendous influence. They provide a pathway to excellence, enabling others to make a real difference. Creative communicators are approachable, intelligent, adaptable, and results-driven. Being influential means people quote you, wish to engage with you, listen to you, and seek your company. Influence is a skill that can be cultivated during training. It differentiates between simply speaking and mastering the art of persuasion. It signifies that you have invested significantly in your personal development and are a lifelong learner.

Embrace the authority of the individuals you represent. You might ask, "Is Sheena the expert at the front of the room?" Whenever you take a seat, people expect that the speaker has more knowledge than they do. They are paying for a shortcut to understanding. When I train others, they compensate for my 30+ years of experience, which empowers them to take action. Can you manage this right now?

Imagine if your company became synonymous with excellence, making your training unforgettable. Do you think Ferrari trainers are well remembered? Why is Ferrari the talk of the world? It is the team, the Ferrari drivers, and the tools, tips, and training provided by world-class trainers. They rely on the insights of specialised coaches, mechanics, and trainers.

Director Note: *Can You Imagine This World-Class Thinking in Your CEO Development?*

Law Six: Does Your Class Allow You to Go the Extra Mile?

You may be surprised to learn that I have a Ferrari in my living room. Each morning, it evokes memories of standing on the track at Monza, Ferrari's home in Milan. I contemplate how I might achieve performance metrics comparable to those of a Ferrari driver. When one thinks of Ferrari, performance and world-class leadership are immediately associated.

Imagine having such excellent positioning. What can Ferrari teach us about performance, and how can you apply these principles to achieve excellence? To win beyond the arena, you need to be an expert in your industry and position yourself as the go-to person. You must maintain a competitive edge in everything you do to become truly exceptional.

At Performance by Design, I have a unique perspective on performance; you might be curious about what inspires me each day. When my feet hit the ground in the morning, I find myself in front of my Ferrari. Every day, I visualise and connect my performance to my Ferrari is that unusual? This distinctive connection gives me the mental readiness to lead the field. What if you had a visual Ferrari in your lounge, speeding from the pit lane to the fast track in business?

So why are we challenged to achieve performance excellence? The world has changed, and so must you.

We find ourselves in a world vastly different from a decade ago. This marks the start of a new chapter in business performance. Your best ideas from five years ago are now outdated. Have you noticed the explosive growth of social media, online shopping, significant technological advancements, a global recession, and a dramatic shift in consumer behaviour?

It is advisable to avoid relying on outdated performance methods. The traditional career path faces obstacles, and businesses now confront an unforeseen new reality. The impact of the office has been felt across all markets, resulting in total disaster and disruption of family life, insolvency, business failures, and significant unemployment. How can you enhance your entrepreneurial skills, embark on a new career, and adopt a fresh mindset to position yourself as a Corporate

Athlete? Of course, it involves high-performance training. Where is your performance gift at this moment?

Director Note: *Inch by Inch is a Cinch, and Yard by Yard is Hard.*

Six Principles of Ferrari Performance

- We evaluate the experts in their brand positioning and their roles.

- We regard world-class performance as when Ferrari dominates the field.

- They have an outstanding brand presence in the market.

- They plan, prepare and practise to be world-class.

- Be that powerful Ferrari engine with eight gears of class.

You also need to position yourself as a high performer. Developing a new formula that enhances your branding and market presence would be ideal. Take the time today to choose a different stage. Are you in first gear? How can you elevate your design training to the next level?

Law Seven: Are You Risking More Than Necessary in Training?

After a brief training session, I contemplated my next move at the summit of the mountain.

Excited, 15 minutes into my ski lesson, I realised I could now do a snowplough. This meant I could stop and start using this technique, which seemed easy. As my friends Lesley and Janey left me to explore the mountain and check out all the runs, I could hear them saying, "You'll be all right, Sheena, as long as you can stop and start."

Was I a mountain person or a valley person? Let's find out.

The second tip I learned was that standing up on my skis slows me down, while bending down allows me to go faster. It all seemed perfectly straightforward. However, this posed a significant risk for me. With a sports background, I was accustomed to training, coaching, and planning, everything an athlete needs to become an elite performer. But there I was, after a brief lesson, preparing for a mountain run. YES, no problem!

I never imagined that taking a risk could lead to dire consequences. Who would have guessed I would race down a mountain at top speed like a Ferrari, covering seven miles without stopping, with no snowplough in sight, bending down or standing up, gathering momentum like a Ferrari on the track?

I found myself lying flat on my back in a field of cows without skis or poles. I had expected a different adventure. This was not an adventure but a serious risk that affected me personally and professionally. As I lay there, 'Snow Patrol' arrived. No, it was not the band Snow Patrol; it was mountain rescue.

"Excuse me, madam. Why are you lying there?"

My response might shock you:

"I'm bloody waiting for a bus. What does it look like? Stupid man!"

Training, whether in sports, music, or business, demands an approach that ensures a risk-free learning environment. All trainees or beginners will acquire the tools, tips, and techniques necessary to achieve successful outcomes in their roles. It is a myth to believe that training can be eliminated in a dynamic economy, as this leads to poor performance, reduced productivity, and suboptimal results. What now, one ski, one glove, is left of my mountain trip?

A lack of training can significantly impact the performance of individuals and companies. I'm sure you agree. Adequate training is the key to achieving an elite level of performance.

This means demonstrating competence in achieving and delivering results, rather than taking risks after just 15 minutes of ski training and ending up in a field of cows.

Director Note: *Concentrate on the Training Task Beyond the Call of Duty*

Law Eight: When Performance Arrives, Preparation Has Gone

Given my limited cooking skills, would Gordon Ramsay's 'Plane Food' training be beneficial?

I was excited about buying my new Hairy Bikers frying pan. To enhance my cooking, I needed a state-of-the-art pan that was non-burning and non-stick. Now that I have the right gear, I'm sharing how I might use it to demonstrate my cooking skills. After all, when you have the right tools, it should be easy.

As my son joined the conversation, I explained how my new frying pan would enhance my cooking skills.

"I'm afraid not, Mum. No new pan will make a difference," he said with a cheeky smile.

What if I tried a new recipe?

"Afraid not, Mum. There's no chance of improvement."

What if I followed the recipe exactly? "There might be a significant improvement."

"I'm afraid not." Mum and my son stood in the doorway laughing. You've guessed it, I don't like being in the kitchen, and I wouldn't say I enjoy cooking, so I don't want to learn or train to be on *MasterChef*.

In my role in HR, I was responsible for the recruitment and selection process, which resulted in new appointments and the implementation of an induction programme. How often do you observe a lack of enthusiasm in new candidates? Does a lack of confidence during training suggest they may learn slowly, become low performers, and require immediate productivity improvements? There's no room in our dynamic economy for inadequate training skills, and it is a myth to think that companies can remain commercially viable without offering training.

During a recent visit to a popular supermarket, I encountered a charming young girl at the checkout who asked me to remove my shopping from my basket, as she thought she might have scanned some items twice. She wasn't sure, and I didn't mind, so I returned five or six items. I reassured her that mistakes can happen. I then enquired if she was entirely new to this role. Her answer took me aback. She had started that day at 1:30 pm. By 4:30 pm, she was unsupervised at the checkout, shame on the supermarket.

Compared to new employees at Boots the Chemist, we had a 12-week programme covering roles, tasks, and responsibilities, which can maximise companies' return on investment. Why do I engage in conversations with high-level business owners who are struggling with the knowledge gap? I can train them to become students of the new economy.

As a CEO or business owner, you must be aware of the critical success factors in your industry and consider designing training that can be delivered during induction for specific roles, as well as for Continuing Professional Development (CPD) and succession planning. These can all maximise the company's return on investment. That's why I converse with high-level C-suite business owners whose lack of knowledge, skills, and expertise concerns me.

My cooking skills have always been a challenge, and I have often been known to almost call the fire brigade. While my friend Catherine was travelling from Inverness back to Glasgow, she asked, "Sheena, should I stop at Marks & Spencer in Dunblane and buy a meal for two that we can enjoy in your lovely garden?" What a fantastic idea! After all, what could go wrong?

Catherine arrived with a meal for two, including a pizza and a bottle of Prosecco. It seemed just perfect. I rubbed my hands in delight, no fuss, no preparation. This was undoubtedly a straightforward approach. Or was it? When people visited, they didn't come to see my house or sample my cooking; they came to see me.

You can imagine my shock and horror as I sat in the garden, enjoying a glass of Prosecco and smelling something burning outside. Oh no, shock and horror, this can't be true! Burning a pizza from a packet? The smell wafting from the kitchen made me jump up quickly. I opened the oven door, and all I saw was smoke and a charred pizza. I thought this oven heated up quickly and seemed to cook faster than the times mentioned on the back of the packet. Would you agree, Catherine? What shall I do now?

Catherine reminded me she had bits and pieces from her Inverness holiday in the car. I looked at the small piece of cheese, a small tomato, and a few slices of cold meat. I'm afraid my son was right to say, "I'm afraid that tools will not improve your cooking skills, Mum." Was there a gap in my culinary skills, a gap in the supermarket's induction, or a more significant gap in business executives' skills?

Director Note: *Excel in the Market with Exceptional Training*

Law Nine: Be a Genius and Showcase Your Mastery in Your Performance

Invest in your people; your customers will sense it, and your business will ultimately reap the rewards. I recalled my coach hitting me on the head with a clipboard to emphasise the significance of training. To be a top performer, mindset and performance must equal a personal best. Can you envision an athlete adopting a careless approach? They strive for excellence at every opportunity and prepare for their performance daily, so I urge you to focus on yourself: who you are, what you do, and, just as importantly, why you are doing it, and why now.

We employ a variety of training methodologies, including action learning, accelerated learning, face-to-face learning, and virtual learning.

Action Learning involves addressing real-life problems and implementing solutions in real-time. It allows learners to gain practical skills and knowledge through direct experience.

Accelerated Learning: This technique utilises strategies to expedite learning, often by engaging multiple senses and accommodating diverse learning styles. It enhances knowledge acquisition, making it more efficient and effective.

Face-to-Face Learning: Traditional in-person training sessions provide direct interaction, immediate feedback, and personal engagement, fostering a strong connection between the trainer and the trainees.

Virtual Learning: Online training is flexible and accessible, allowing learners to engage from anywhere. It utilises digital tools and platforms to provide interactive and engaging content.

As a training student, you should constantly strive to be the best you can be and aspire to become world-class. This involves mastering your teaching content and continually improving your methods and approaches. I am sharing practical ideas, concepts, and strategies to help you disseminate your knowledge and expand your business internationally.

Focusing on these aspects can enhance your training capabilities, motivate others, and have a significant impact on your field. Embrace lifelong learning and self-improvement; you will be well-prepared to lead and effectively influence others.

Begin your journey to becoming a world-class trainer today. Embrace innovative learning methodologies to enhance your skills and broaden your influence. Share your expertise and elevate your business to new heights. Let's transform your training into a global success story.

Director Note: *Become a Global Star in Quality Design Training*

Law Ten: Create an Outstanding Training Session How?

To be an exceptional trainer, one must possess a genuine passion for the role and be prepared to make sacrifices for personal and professional improvement. So, what common factor unites most trainers? There are various types of trainers: formal, casual, humorous, and profound. The possibilities are endless. What suits you best, and how do you categorise them? When presenting to a board of directors, we demonstrate that we have achieved a result, which enables them to reward us. Another trainer might share creativity, innovation, and ideas. It is essential to provide the board and shareholders with information and give them a compelling reason to embrace that idea and make it their own.

Director's Note: *By Offering Public Speaking Training, I Can Demonstrate the Value and Return on Investment of Being Viewed as an Authority.*

Design, Develop and Deliver a Blockbuster Cycle

Design Cycle Guide

9.00 am 9.30 am. Introductions and Course Objectives

- Exercise Introductions
- Slide Course Objectives

9.30 am 10.15 am. Skills for Effective Training

- Slide Retention rates, why train? What is training for
- Exercise - Benefits of training
- Exercise - Training skills
- Slide Effective training skills

10.15 am 11.15 am. Training Methods and Effective Communication

- Slide Training methods
- Exercise Perception
- Exercise Listening skills
- Exercise Giving instructions

11.15 am 12.30 pm. Instructional Techniques

- Slides Instructional techniques and question techniques
- Exercise Instructional techniques

1.00 pm 2.00 pm. The Training Cycle

- Slide Training Cycle
- Exercise Induction training the sales assistant

2.00 pm 3.00 pm. Setting Training Objectives

- Slide Programme planning, Aspiring objectives, and measurement criteria
- Exercise Induction training outline plan

3.00 pm 4.15 pm. Preparing and Delivering a Training Session

- Exercise Preparing a training session and training topic
- Exercise Deliver a training session and review

4.15 pm 4.30 pm. Action Planning and Course Feedback

- Slide Course Objectives
- Exercise Action plan
- Exercise Course feedback and evaluation

A master trainer creates a scene where learning becomes performance. These Directors Notes offer your next direction in crafting training with clarity and class.

Director Note

Chapter 5: Training by Craft

- Training is the script for transformation. The best directors train minds to think, act, and perform with excellence.

- Simplify one training module to deliver 10x clarity.

- Create one new tool to amplify learning impact.

- Rehearse your next delivery with world-class precision.

- Remove jargon elevate every word to world stage standard.

Sheena

Say Yes to Reinvention with Design

Chapter 6
Crafting Enchanting Customer Experiences

"Customer service is no longer enough enchantment is the new standard." Sheena Walker

Delivering exceptional customer experiences fosters brand loyalty. Satisfied customers are more likely to return for repeat business and become long-term advocates for your service. In a competitive marketplace, outstanding customer experiences can set your business apart. They act as a unique selling point that attracts and retains customers. Happy customers often spend more, make larger purchases, and are more inclined to recommend your business to others, thereby increasing sales and revenue.

Ipsos MORI, a renowned global market research company, specialises in identifying and understanding the key factors that shape customers' preferences and decisions. Their studies have uncovered essential habits and qualities that customers value in products, services, and brands. These findings reveal that frequently cited service habits, such as fulfilling promises, ensuring prompt service, and consistently offering genuine smiles along with polite expressions of 'please' and 'thank you', have a significant impact on customers' choices. Such practices form the foundation of an exceptional customer experience and are crucial for retaining customers and encouraging them to return.

Think back to the last time you delivered truly exceptional customer service. Did you receive feedback? What do your clients say about your services? What do they say you excel at? Imagine knowing exactly which habits capture your customers' attention and have them praising your business. The reality is that achieving this is relatively straightforward. Exceptional service costs nothing, but its value is immense.

As the chief executive, chairperson, leader, or manager, you must make your customers feel valued by providing a unique, tailored experience. This inspires them to share their positive experiences and promote your brand. In the corporate world, I trained my teams to champion change in every aspect of the customer experience.

Consistently delivering exceptional service can position you to dominate your market, yielding significant returns on investment. Companies like BMW and Amazon employ just-in-time principles in customer service. This ensures resources are used efficiently, products are available in the right quantities at the right time, and customer needs are met, providing unmatched market positioning.

This chapter outlines nine habits to enhance your brand and skills while ensuring an exceptional customer experience. Building a strong brand identity that resonates with customers is essential to fostering loyalty. Cultivating good corporate manners means developing practical skills and maintaining daily dedication to outstanding service.

Habit One: Securing Customer Approval is the Path Forward

Many people experience poor customer service without understanding the reasons behind it. What drives customers away, and how can this be changed? Imagine having top-performing individuals in your organisation who excel in customer service.

During my time at Boots PLC, customer experience was paramount. Everyone, from top management to frontline staff, was committed to the customer strategy. Recruitment, induction, training, and succession planning were all essential to maintaining the brand's professional identity and enhancing performance.

Senior leaders, in particular, have a pivotal influence on a company's strategic direction. For instance, the head of customer service has a major impact on the overall customer experience. Recognising and supporting such individuals with the right resources is essential to achieving strategic objectives and accurately measuring success.

Delivering excellence through a "celebrity level" of service and performance has proven to be a powerful route to success. Initially, some managers struggled with this concept. A turning point came when I drew parallels between customer service and the discipline of sports champions, highlighting the need for CEOs and leaders to model these skills in order to influence staff behaviour.

I took a proactive approach, consistently volunteering for training and embracing new opportunities. I vividly recall when Cap Gemini introduced innovative coaching methods to enhance performance. Eager to contribute, I sought a role in floor training as a performance coach. My determination to be fully engaged saw me join the team quickly, facilitating and educating our managers. This proved pivotal in empowering us to maintain a competitive edge.

Director Note: *Are You Taking More Risks Than Necessary?*

In life's grand theatre, every customer interaction requires careful consideration of risks. Pursuing greatness often means stepping beyond the comfort of convention, risking more than is comfortable. Yet in pushing those boundaries, we often find the greatest growth, understanding, and the potential for an extraordinary customer experience.

Habit Two: Build Your Reputation, Become Notable in Your Industry

Some business owners seem to attract clients effortlessly. Everyone knows their name, and they have as much business as they can handle. But how do they do it?

Living in the picturesque countryside just 12 miles from the renowned Gleneagles Hotel is a privilege. It's where I enjoy coffee, meet clients for inspiring discussions, and explain how I can help them stand out in ways that make them impossible to ignore.

What is it about Gleneagles? It's the location, the ambience, the staff, their tone of voice, and the way the experience makes me feel so welcome. Is Gleneagles famous? Yes, it's where celebrities go. It has hosted the Ryder Cup, boasts an exclusive membership, a prime location, and offers incomparable service.

Some businesses, like Gleneagles, effortlessly attract clients and customers. They don't cold-call or rely on advertising, yet they are consistently featured in newspapers and magazines. Everyone knows their name, and they enjoy all the business they can manage. They may not be famous like film stars or world-class athletes, but they are well-known enough to be top of mind when people search for a product or service.

Would you like to adopt the mindset of being 'somewhat famous' when customers approach you? This may require a new way of thinking and a fresh approach to planning your customer experience strategy. Recently, a friend suggested we meet for coffee at Starbucks. Without realising it, I scrunched up my face and replied, "Starbucks?" My friend laughed and said, "You're getting too accustomed to Gleneagles for coffee." And I had to ask myself, why did I have that reaction?

Customers often describe their experiences as either exceptional or disappointing, rarely something in between. Dissatisfaction can occur across a wide range of places, from hospitals, hotels, and garages to restaurants. It can also apply to products and services that fail to deliver, or to delays and long waiting times. These frustrations, whether poor service, slow delivery, or unmet expectations, erode trust and loyalty. This is why it's so important to create delightful customer moments and consistently deliver a five-star experience.

When was the last time you experienced something like Gleneagles? Do you remember giving feedback to the company and feeling genuinely appreciated? More importantly, do your customers feel valued after dealing with your business? Achieving five-star service is not simply a matter of financial investment, it starts with cultivating the right mindset. It means adopting strategies that make customers feel exceptional, going beyond the transaction and turning them into brand advocates.

Director Note: *Delivering on a Promise The Heart of Customer Experience Excellence*

Habit Three: Embracing Our Inner Superstar Qualities

Within each of us are extraordinary qualities waiting to be released. Don't believe it? It's about engaging in meaningful conversations, choosing words that truly matter, words that make customers feel valued and inspire loyalty.

Once, while in a checkout queue, I had an unexpected moment of amusement. It had been ages since anyone had affectionately called me "darling". Can you imagine? Here I was, greeted by a checkout operator using that endearing term. While it might seem trivial, the effect was memorable. Perhaps he uses it a hundred times a day, but that doesn't diminish its charm. It's a reminder that small, personal touches can resonate deeply. As the saying goes, "Meet someone without a smile, and give them one of yours."

Do you have strategies that allow your customers to feel exceptional? Think about well-known brands like Nike, McDonald's, Ferrero Rocher, Prada, or Apple. Their identities are instantly recognisable because they have built strong brand images and become the preferred choice for certain customers.

Is dominating the market the only way to succeed? Surprisingly, focusing on customers and service can be even more powerful. How can you reach that level of recognition? In today's economy, executives, entrepreneurs, and start-ups are leading in different market sectors. The challenge is targeting the right prospects and positioning yourself for success.

Take my recent trip with LNER as an example. Despite weather-related delays, the service from London to

Scotland was outstanding. The train manager kept passengers informed throughout, which made a big difference. When I realised, I would miss my connecting train in Edinburgh, I panicked, mainly because I'd be alone, in difficult weather, at 1:30 a.m. But my fears were quickly eased thanks to the staff's calm and attentive approach.

The staff provided outstanding service by arranging a taxi to meet me at the station and take me home. What could have been a potential disaster turned into a commendable experience. Rather than merely meeting expectations, the company went far beyond the call of duty. This perfectly encapsulates why I am sharing it with you, and it assures my continued support of the train company. Furthermore, due to their customer service policy, I was pleasantly reminded that I could claim a refund for my ticket because of the train delay of over an hour.

Imagine creating unforgettable moments within your organisation that stay in people's minds, compelling them to recommend you to others.

Director Note: *Honour Your Commitment Does Your Brand Elicit a 'Yes'?*

What would people say about you? How exceptional is your performance? How remarkable are your contributions? How can you personally and professionally uphold your commitment to customer service tomorrow? Challenge yourself to ask three people to describe your qualities, you may be surprised by their perspectives.

Habit Four: How Can You Cultivate a Unique Market Niche?

Are you visualising a high standard of customer experience, service, and expectations as essential right now? I have become increasingly critical of the patient and customer service standards in various sectors. Staff recruitment and the lack of proper training are, frankly, shockingly poor, which affects many organisations.

We live in exciting times, and your organisation has the opportunity to deliver a service that exceeds all expectations. Think briefly of our world-class athletes, Andy Murray, Ronaldo, Messi. Would they ever dare not to train? To play below par, neglect practice, and then perform poorly on the pitch? Would it be tolerated? Would the manager have something to say? Absolutely. The same applies to our organisations: we must raise our game and achieve victory beyond the arena. But how do we truly realise our potential?

Consider public relations strategies that focus on your target audience, think about the magazines they read, the events they attend, and how you can connect your brand to professional credibility. Enhancing your credibility is one of the most effective ways to establish yourself as an expert. This requires drawing on your deep understanding of clients, customers, and your industry, knowledge your competitors simply cannot match.

Do you sometimes see companies you believe lack your skills becoming market leaders?

Why? Is it because they have mastered the art of marketing themselves?

Director Note: *Keep Your Presence and Your Voice Leading in the Market*

Speaking is one of the most valuable skills in business today. Communicating your message clearly and engaging in impactful conversations about your services is essential. If there is one word that defines excellent brand identity and positioning, it is *visibility*.

Habit Five: Celebrities Dream Big and Start Small

Renowned individuals understand the importance of delivering five-star, celebrity-level service, not just for customers, but also for employees. These high standards directly influence an organisation's overall success. My mantra of "five stars" is present in all my roles, and I often draw on my athletic background to deliver high-impact human performance training for elite clients and companies.

I have successfully applied these principles to achieve a modest level of recognition while enhancing customer experiences.

So, how do ordinary people end up connected with celebrities like Oprah Winfrey, Warren Buffett, or even the iconic characters from *The Wizard of Oz*? What lifts them from modest beginnings to first-class status? Harvard University research into individuals from business, sport, and media who achieved remarkable success revealed common factors behind their rise.

The key finding? We all possess a similar blend of talents and weaknesses, but those who stand out know how to maximise their strengths and minimise the impact of their weaknesses. If I asked you to name your greatest talent, could you? Take a moment to consider it.

Like elite athletes, these individuals understand the specific steps required to build their success. They recognise how their emotions, mindset, and preparation directly influence the quality of their work. Companies thrive when they manage themselves and their talents effectively. Whatever your industry, be innovative, creative, and deliberate. Encourage your team to think like designers, and don't be afraid to take calculated risks to advance your career or entrepreneurial ambitions.

Director Note: *Capitalise on Your Talents with Grand Ideas*

Habit Six: Develop a Distinctive Personality and Core Values

Are you the employer of choice, the company people aspire to work for?

Your priority must be to uphold your values and beliefs. Many organisations offer a list of services but lack clear positioning, making it difficult to stand out in a crowded market. The key lies in presenting them differently.

Brands like BMW, McDonald's, and Apple have unmistakable identities, we know exactly what they represent. Do you understand what your service stands for? Do your employees? Do they take pride in saying, "I work for an outstanding company, and our product is the best on the market"? Or do they undermine the brand with constant negativity?

A prime example of an employer of choice is the BBC programme *The Firm*, which provides an in-depth look at the life and work of Anmer Anwar, a prominent lawyer from Glasgow. Anwar is a skilled legal professional and a notable British political activist who actively engages in various socio-political issues. His dedication to assisting families struggling to make their voices heard within the legal system is admirable. However, what impressed me most was his remarkable blend of personal empathy and professionalism in managing these high-profile cases.

Anwar's expertise encompasses a variety of legal services, including criminal defence, appeals, and parole matters. His stated values and beliefs set him apart, as he generously shares his knowledge, skills, and insights with his team. This positions him as a prominent figure in both the legal and political spheres.

Richard Branson sincerely believes that caring for and supporting your staff creates a positive and nurturing work environment where performance issues are rare. When employees feel valued, supported, and motivated, they naturally tend to perform at their best, go the extra mile, and show unwavering dedication. This, in turn, fosters a culture of excellence where productivity increases and both the team's and the organisation's success grow.

A culture of excellence is not always the case. Today, I began looking for a trip to Australia.

I called a well-known company, and an automated answering machine informed me that I was number thirty-seven in the queue and that the waiting time was 44 minutes. I reached out to the other eight branches, and I received similar responses. We are not in the COVID era, so what is the excuse for the inferior customer service now? Will I use this company? I don't think I need to ask you that. Will this company flourish? I think not.

Maintaining your values and brand should focus on a transformative mission: to elevate executives from essential expertise to the peak of authority by instilling world-class values and unmatched beliefs. While this statement may seem simple, its implications are significant. I express this clearly because I want my audience to have precise expectations of what my brand represents and what I will deliver. I firmly believe in the superiority of my service, and I don't hesitate to assert that in my biography. My commitment to excellence drives me to provide expertise and transformation that distinguish my brand, ensuring that my clients receive the best possible service.

Many companies lack a branding or personality strategy, causing them to blend in with millions of others in the market. How can you provide more exceptional value through your customer service and by training your staff to think and act differently in your services?

What is your brand identity? What do you stand for? Does your staff understand your company's brand positioning? If not, it's time to start. What if you were remembered for your positioning statement? Would it reflect your services? In 25 words or fewer, who are you? What is your area of expertise?

Director Note: *Become the Greatest by Performing at Your Best*

Habit 7: Excel as an Oscar Winner in the Marketplace

This week, I was interviewed by a leading firm in the United States about "Dare to Be Different." What did I do differently, and how did I stand out? My approach to design thinking is centred on generating brilliant ideas and employing innovative strategies. I deliver these as my signature model, pushing the boundaries of commercially viable performance.

How can you leverage your modest fame in business? You should embody your narrative. You are your business; showcasing and utilising all the personalities involved is essential as it grows. Your personality matters, even if you believe it isn't fascinating or distinctive enough. What does distinctive truly mean? You are enough to make your business shine. Everyone possesses a unique point of difference: what's yours?

What does it take to get noticed in your market? Once you understand and accept that you are the essence of your business, you can be bolder and less fearful of standing out in a crowd, thereby creating loyal fans. More clients who love you as fans are likely to be faithful and will pay more to buy from you. And what's the result? Being a business celebrity doesn't mean you have to handle every aspect of your business, but it does reflect your personality and approach in everything you undertake.

A small business needs a personality just as much as a larger business, and the results are the same: more loyal clients buying from you because of who you are.

If you don't consistently keep a straightforward businessperson in mind, all your business actions will seem disjointed. If you run your own small business, you can easily manage this personally. However, in a larger company, your personality must be documented and formalised into a procedure.

Don't let this diminish its power and impact. Instead, allow it to strengthen the business personality by reinforcing and enriching the personalities of your team managers and staff.

Social media blurs the boundaries between business and 'real life,' so you must confront and utilise this shift.

While extensive theoretical knowledge is valuable, true growth comes from your brand story. Without personalisation and achieving commercial success, you will remain stagnant despite your expertise.

Be authentic and daring. People will notice you for it and will want to purchase from you.

Director Note: *Be Persistent in Your Passion and Personality*

Habit 8: Why Customers Don't Choose You, Is This Serious?

Seems serious? Employing 'Radar Thinking': how can a series of complaints and issues evolve into a five-star service? Renowned customer experience expert Shep Hyken advises against companies boasting about their large or busy customer complaint departments, as it instantly signals poor service.

Consider the 'Radar Thinking' concept: What happens if a recurring issue at work remains unresolved? How can you turn challenges into customer service successes and gain customer approval? Reflect on customers' difficulties with delivery times and costs, as well as the need for specialised staff training in handling complaints.

Does your company manage complaints through a dedicated department or a specialised team, or are issues addressed as they arise? Sometimes, the stories I encounter seem unbelievable, almost mythical. Those who raise complaints about a company with a large complaints department might find it less appealing as an employer. Escalated complaints highlight shortcomings in leadership, processes, and systems, exposing gaps in customer strategy and management.

Our TV screens inundate us daily with issues faced by various sectors, including the NHS, rail travel, education departments, Royal Mail, and much of the public sector. The NHS, in particular, presents a significant narrative, with continuous reports of staff shortages, overcrowding, and other challenges dominating the headlines.

What if redesigning services and personnel could bring about change? Enhancing waiting times might lead to more efficient and effective service, improved patient care initiatives, and transformed staff management.

In essence, 'Radar Thinking' represents a proactive and meticulous approach to managing customer complaints. It emphasises attentiveness, analysis, detail orientation, swift action, and continuous responsiveness for an optimal customer experience.

Director Note: *Embracing a New Strategy Respond Faster, Resolve Better and Retain Loyalty*

Habit 9: Three Magic Words for Handling Complaints

Often, companies neglect or show disinterest when addressing complaints. Imagine encountering an issue without a prompt resolution. Picture this scenario: a customer returns goods without a receipt, only to receive a robotic response citing company policy.

"No receipt, no refund." This is a common occurrence in many retail environments, leading to customer frustration, annoyance, and anger. The absence of proof of purchase creates a challenging and distressing situation that can potentially drive customers to boycott your service.

Let's explore a new approach to exceptional service by fostering meaningful conversations and cultivating rapport and trust. I've had considerable success coaching my staff using the "Feel, Felt, and Found" technique when handling angry customers.

Acknowledging the customer's feelings with "I'm sorry that you feel that way" aligns you with their emotions, demonstrating empathy and understanding. This thoughtful response, along with sharing your own experiences of similar feelings, highlights your emotional connection. This method possesses considerable power in communication, reflecting expertise and problem-solving skills. Adopting this three-step "FFF" strategy distinguishes your approach to resolving complaints.

'Radar Thinking' epitomises a proactive and meticulous approach to addressing customer grievances. It emphasises the importance of attentiveness, thorough analysis, prompt action, and continuous responsiveness to ensure an optimal customer experience. This comprehensive strategy guarantees a customer-centric resolution process.

A Radar's approach to customer complaints employs a systematic method that effectively addresses customers' concerns. It includes several key elements, such as promptly recognising, acknowledging, and understanding the customer's complaint, its significance, and its impact on the customer experience.

Evaluate the complaint carefully, considering various factors such as the nature of the issue and the customer's perspective, to establish the most appropriate course of action.

Director Note: *Deliver a Customer Experience Using a Feel-Felt-Found Approach*

Every customer moment is a live scene. And you, the Director, have the power to elevate it into something unforgettable. Use these notes to refine the experience.

Director Note

Chapter 6: Customer Enchantment

- Service is not a role; it's a performance. In the director's chair, customer experience becomes customer theatre personal, memorable, elite.
- Review one customer touchpoint and elevate it too unforgettable.
- Respond to one piece of feedback with leadership presence.
- Script a moment of surprise for your next client interaction.
- Build loyalty through one genuine, unscripted gesture.

Sheena

Say Yes to Extraordinary Customer Experience

Chapter 7
The Master Mentor Machine

"Mentoring is the VIP pass to wisdom, experience, and the fast lane to your podium." Sheena Walker

Warren Buffett is renowned for his profound insights into life and success. He is also a remarkable mentor who teaches others how to improve their performance. As a world-class authority in business, he knows that developing skills in finance, sales, customer service, and leadership is essential in a challenging trading environment.

How Can You Be That Great Advancement?

To maximise your business's productivity, emulate Warren Buffett and guide your team towards achieving world-class performance.

Have you studied everything like a scientist while approaching it like a champion? Champions are known for concentrating their energy and focusing on what they desire with an intensity that borders on obsession. They block out anything or anyone that threatens that focus. While average people attribute success to luck or intelligence, champions are committed to developing an elite team around them. They keep digging until they discover that vein of gold in their people.

Which one do you identify as, average or world-class?

Currently, there is a lack of clarity regarding training, coaching, and mentoring. Most people assume these skills are equivalent, but they are not. In many companies, individuals with little to no experience take on roles for which they are underqualified. This happens because the professional development sector is a billion-pound industry filled with self-proclaimed experts.

In one of my business roles, where I collaborate with clinicians and allied medical professionals, strict governance by the British Medical Council is essential for the practice of medicine. Can you imagine visiting your GP or a doctor who has not received professional mentoring since graduating from university? In sport, governing bodies also validate and accredit coaching programmes that instil high-quality standards among professionals.

In the business world, mentoring is often provided without formal training or validation for several reasons. Informal mentoring arises from personal relationships and connections. Many mentors are experienced professionals who voluntarily share their knowledge and insights with others. Their organic nature may not include formal training or validation processes, as their professional qualifications are sufficient.

Throughout my career, I have served as both a mentee and a mentor. What truly matters is a genuine desire for success and a clear commitment to the process. Mentoring significantly enhances individuals' productivity and effectiveness, providing them with a competitive advantage. If you lack a competitive edge, what is the point of what you are doing?

This chapter will present the fundamentals of being an exceptional *Mentoring Machine* by illustrating mentoring standards and mastery questions.

Sheena L.C. Walker

The Body of a Ferrari with a Bicycle Mind

I am standing in the pit lane at Monza, the home of Ferrari. I asked myself: how does Ferrari raise the bar on performance? How do they develop the skills necessary to win in Formula One?

Imagine you are a Ferrari racing driver. Can you visualise the body of a Ferrari? A Ferrari body typically embodies the attributes and characteristics associated with high performance, sleek, powerful, and attractive, often evoking comparisons to the design and speed of the car itself.

When was the last time you stood in the boardroom with the mind of a bicycle? Imagine if everything you did to develop your people was automatic and effortless, becoming second nature. It is time to consider lubricating your body and mind so that they function more smoothly. Can you envision the attributes and characteristics associated with the design of a Ferrari?

Would you dare to take a different approach to performance? Mentoring is increasingly being recognised worldwide and can be found in many organisations, from the private to the public sectors. Is mentoring done well, or is it mediocre and in need of improvement? Why would you not strive to improve? The Ferrari formula is a journey to a new destination, taking people from the pit lane to the fast track. However, obstacles and stumbling blocks can impede our journey. Our brain operates with automatic and effortless proficiency, like riding a bicycle; once learned, it becomes second nature.

Director Note: *It's Time to Leave the Pit Lane, Step onto The Performance Track, and Drive Your Success with My Ferrari Tool Box*

Greatness Starts Outside Your Comfort Zone

As a mentor, cultivate a passion for performance and strive for greatness, which often begins outside your comfort zone. Stepping beyond your comfort zone involves venturing into unfamiliar and insecure experiences. It requires embracing challenges, risks, and situations that may initially feel uncomfortable in order to promote growth and learning.

Effective mentoring emphasises a commitment to human relationships and the resources necessary to assist less experienced individuals in achieving success and fulfilment in their professional pursuits.

Stepping out of their comfort zones was not typically an issue for Dan Walker, a Channel Five presenter, writer, and broadcaster, and his fellow presenter, Helen Skelton. However, the challenge took on a different shape as they ventured into the Pennines, undertaking the task of crossing from one side of the mountain to the other on a rope. Dan's hesitation pushed him out of his comfort zone during this mountain expedition, and he admitted to having a "fear of heights." Helen's quick wit and calming voice motivated him to confront the challenge. Dan, who had less experience, received guidance from a more seasoned individual who supported him at every stage of his development. Imagine applying this mindset in your own life. Regardless of the style, mentoring is an excellent way to learn swiftly. Supporting another person's growth requires a significant amount of time and energy.

However, mentors should avoid an authoritarian approach and instead act as teachers and educators. Great mentors will discuss the diagnosis and prognosis to impart new skills for future roles.

One of the best ways to uncover the mentor within you is to reflect on your past experiences as a mentor. Dan would have experienced the expertise of the mountaineering team first-hand, selected for their knowledge and industry background, ensuring they possessed the qualifications and formal training to support this learning experience for him.

Director Note: *Elite Results Begin by Refining Complexity. This Method Transforms Ambitious Goals into Actionable, Elegant Steps*

The Simplicity of Mentoring Sophistication

Six key traits that mountaineering mentors possess make them exceptionally effective at nurturing talent and fostering the development of others. Let's explore how you can integrate these traits into your teaching.

One: Empathy and Understanding

Successful mentors empathise with their mentees, understand their challenges, aspirations, and unique circumstances, and provide personalised guidance to foster a supportive environment.

Two: Active Listening

Mentoring champions are adept listeners. They attentively consider the mentee's concerns, questions, and feedback, enabling them to provide relevant advice and insights.

Three: Experience and Expertise

Influential mentors possess a solid foundation of experience and expertise in their field. This knowledge enables them to share practical advice, industry insights, and valuable lessons, contributing to the mentee's growth.

Four: Openness to Learning

The best mentors understand that learning is a two-way street. They remain open to learning from their mentees' perspectives and experiences, creating a mutually beneficial relationship.

Five: Guidance and Feedback

Mentoring champions are recognised for offering constructive guidance and candid feedback. They help individuals set goals, track progress, and navigate challenges by providing actionable suggestions and evaluations.

Six: Empowerment and Advocacy

Mentoring champions empower mentees to take charge of their development. They advocate for their mentees' success, creating opportunities and fostering growth and networks.

Director Note: *Intentionally Shape Your Mentoring with Six Champion Elements*

Every New Mentor Wants to Discover the Essential Questions

As a mentor, you should understand the five types of questions: curious, clarifying, possibility, genius, and golden questions. How many times have you heard this in conversation? Do you hear people say, "This has been the worst time in business ever"? You can change this mindset now by adopting fresh ideas, posing insightful questions, and sharing your expertise.

Numerous mentoring questions exist. Mastery questions are akin to an iPhone app released only a few years ago. For novices, this approach may have a different impact than it does for those with more experience, who ask intentional questions to foster individual development.

The Luxury Brand Formula

First thing in the morning, I admire my model Ferrari in my lounge. It brings back memories of standing on the track at Monza, listening to the racing drivers and asking, "How do I transition from the pit lane to the fast track of performance?"

Essentially, the journey of the Ferrari from the pit lane to the high-performance track stems from a holistic approach that includes engineering excellence, a skilled workforce, relentless innovation, and a strong commitment to its racing heritage and brand values. This concept is equally relevant in the business world.

How does one move from an expert to an authority in the luxury marketplace? Is there more to learn than anticipated?

Genius Questions for Luxury Brands

Genius questions in mentoring are thought-provoking and inquiry-driven, stimulating critical thinking, creativity, and profound insights. This approach encourages clients to explore their ideas, assumptions, and potential solutions, fostering a more meaningful and enriching mentorship experience within the luxury market.

Ferrari's brand positioning symbolises aspirational luxury and offers a unique experience. Its luxury brand strategy has enabled Ferrari to consistently dominate its global status and achieve outstanding performance in both the commercial and automotive sectors. Ferrari positions itself as a prestigious luxury brand, and its association with motorsport further elevates its status, appealing to discerning customers.

Establish areas of exclusivity by asking five positioning questions to enhance allure and prestige.

Q: How can your staff achieve exceptional performance in delivering that experience?

Ferrari's image is recognised globally, and its marketing contributes to its success. Review your client's brand marketing and social media campaigns.

Q: Does my product control the market, and is it priced at a premium?

Ferrari approaches sponsorship and customer engagement by personalising experiences. How can you capitalise on the high-end market for your product and services?

Q: How can you access a new market?

Imagine bold new ideas and directions in the business world. Ferrari's red brand presence has extended into other segments of the commercial world.

Q: How can you enhance your business presence through new joint ventures to ensure commercial viability and success?

Explore uncharted territories by considering innovative technology or concepts that provide advanced features to enhance performance.

Q: Kindly elaborate on your business, brand, productivity, and strategy for enhancing brand identity in your sector with immediate Ferrari recognition.

How? By making exclusivity and rarity hallmarks of incomparability.

Questions for Mentoring Directors of Luxury Brands

I aspire to be a luxury brand, collaborating with a client who wishes to lead the industry. How can we tap into an incomparable market?

Pose questions that help identify gaps in performance using a scoring system of one to ten:

- Where is the client currently regarding their performance?

- What is essential to address in your business at this moment?

- What has stopped you from resolving the issues?

- What will happen in the future without mentoring?

- What decisions are you currently making for the business?

Celebrity Mentoring Renowned Brands

How do you make a CEO feel valued when you start impactful discussions? By inspiring conversations as a celebrity mentor, your clients will find you brilliant.

The same could be said for a rock band; one of my favourites is *Take That*. Before their stage performance, they plan, prepare, and practise to make a lasting impact. Could you achieve this level of influence?

Imagine mentoring staff like a rock star, guiding them to become world-class and command the stage at every performance. The same principle applies to business: commanding a room in any setting is essential. If this marks a new beginning for you and your CEO, ask thoughtful questions to uncover the root of their challenges or underperformance.

Questions that Spark Performance Discussions

Curious questions in mentoring are thoughtful, open-ended inquiries that encourage executives to reflect, explore, and expand their thinking. They foster deeper conversations, promote self-discovery, and help mentees gain insight and clarity regarding their goals and challenges. Additionally, asking curious questions is an effective way to understand why staff members may be underperforming.

A performance scale ranging from one to ten, indicating poor to excellent performance with varying degrees in between, can be utilised to assess different performance aspects based on the context. The higher the score, the better the performance. This approach is a thoughtful way to begin planning.

I want to ask you a few questions:

- What have you achieved this week?

- How can you reverse this situation and achieve better results next time?

- Are you seeking mentorship on this, or are you simply sharing it?

- May I share an observation that could be helpful?

- Could we agree on the following steps for success?

Director Note: *Self-Mastery Sharpens Every Conversation. Start by Asking Yourself the Right Questions Daily*

Mastermind Mentoring

Andrew Carnegie, a steel magnate from Scotland, discovered an excellent way to maximise performance. He believed that participants quickly became powerful, influential, and knowledgeable when leaders shared their specialised topics with mentees through mastermind groups.

While companies conduct weekly meetings, many are disorganised and lack the qualities of a true mastermind. Napoleon viewed masterminding as a means for experts to foster passion and confidence through associating with a peer group.

Napoleon Hill, Carnegie's mentee and the author of *Think and Grow Rich*, believed that a group of like-minded individuals could significantly enhance one another's success in their industry.

Mastermind success operates on three guiding principles for breaking performance boundaries: a blueprint encompassing processes, systems, and evaluation. This type of group offers a platform for collaboration, idea sharing, and joint problem-solving among peers. Such groups often provide diverse perspectives, which can lead to innovative solutions.

Two mastermind groups, the Academy of Chief Executives and Vistage, provide distinctive insights into resources and skills across various industries. Can you imagine being part of a group of energised individuals committed to improving their lives personally and professionally? Without such groups, individuals may lack the support, fresh insights, and external feedback necessary to contribute to their personal and business growth.

Director Note: *Do you have Meetings or Mastermind groups?*

Which option could be commercially viable? Your specific needs and preferences will dictate whether you work in a group or independently. What would now provide you and your staff with incredible personal and professional benefits?

Three Key Influences for Producers

One: Mastermind groups operate most effectively when structured; however, they must remain flexible and responsive to the group's needs. The key is to generate consistent and impactful results for members by reframing questions and approaching them with positive intent.

Question: What is our mission, and what do we need to achieve today?

Commitment is a strong example of a business scenario or sporting situation.

Two: How Do We Move from the Starting Block to the Fast Track?

Your group should comprise like-minded individuals who share similar values and beliefs and are committed to pushing performance boundaries. Diverse perspectives can lead to enlightening experiences for members. However, if individuals join the group with significantly different viewpoints, they may struggle to establish common ground, which can hinder the group's progress.

Question: What is the objective of this group, and what do you hope to accomplish?

Discuss the experiences and resources that each person contributes to the group.

Three: First, Be the Best, Then Be First

What is the meeting format, dates, times, and locations?

Choose a captivating name for the group.

Establish the ground rules.

Member discussion: three minutes each, promptly.

Ask what their three top priorities are.

What are they currently working on? What are their intentions?

Refer to previous questions about their challenges, etc.

Director Note: *Mastering Your Conversational Gears Like a Ferrari Elevates Speed, Precision, and Distinction in Mentoring*

Mentors Who Take Centre Stage in the Boardroom

Are you the focal point of your boardroom? If given the choice, would you feel excited if your presence defined your quality? What comes to mind when you hear the term *centrepiece*? Perhaps you think of an artist's work, someone creative who has made their mark on the world?

Did Michelangelo, Rembrandt, Picasso, Van Gogh, and Leonardo da Vinci spring to mind? You would be correct. They created masterpieces despite numerous stumbling blocks. Does this sound familiar in your world?

Leonardo da Vinci took four years to paint the *Mona Lisa* without anyone to pose thought-provoking questions or spark a conversation. How will you demonstrate your authority in your role so that people will stop and think, *"Why didn't I consider that?"*

Excellent mentoring fosters high performance in staff, enhances a product or service, and yields a significant return on investment. Would you follow someone you did not respect or like? We both know the answer.

Visualise yourself as a mentor for executive presence, guiding essential aspects such as communication, style, body language, personal branding, and emotional intelligence to help mentees achieve success. Charismatic, passionate mentors with executive presence find it easier to cultivate that essential relationship.

Andy Lothian, CEO of Insights, a global company based in Dundee, demonstrates this superbly as a conversationalist with passion, energy, and drive. This is undoubtedly a unique differentiator for Andy and his international team. Do your skills match, and exceed, all others?

Director Note: *Investing in Self-Mastery Makes Conversations Purposeful and Focused on Becoming That Focal Point. What Questions Might You Ask Yourself Each Day?*

Self-Mastery Question

When you think of Leonardo da Vinci and others who have made their mark, what were the key challenges they faced? As a speaker and mentor, have you experienced similar thoughts? Some of the most common issues I hear are:

- Staying focused requires effort.
- I have no one to hold me accountable for my actions.
- I'm looking forward to that opportunity.
- I'm busier than ever and don't have time to train.
- I currently feel uncertain about my finances.
- I require assistance with all my services.
- I am still determining what my purpose is.

Questions to Consider When Selecting a Mentor

- What is your area of expertise?
- Could your area of expertise assist me at this moment?
- Could you please share the current results of your case studies?
- Where did you receive your mentor training? (This could be a sensitive topic.)

Director Note: *Elite Mentors Lead with Class, Character, and Presence, Leaving a Legacy Shaped by Preparation and Self-Mastery.*

I have shared a teaching masterclass designed to fast-track your performance. One effective way to pursue excellence is to delve deeper into calibrating yourself and expanding your brand identity to achieve an unmatched market presence.

Director Note

Chapter 7: Magnetic Mentoring

- Mentoring is mastery passed on. Directors don't just advise they shape legacy. Let your presence lead and your wisdom land.

- Identify one person to champion this month.

- Share a story, not just advice.

- Design a "Mentor Moment" in your schedule weekly.

- Ask yourself: "What would my mentor say about my current decisions?"

Sheena

Say Yes to Playing Big or Not at All

Chapter 8
The Prosperity of Wealth and Wellbeing

"True prosperity is not just measured in numbers, but in the energy, clarity, and vitality you carry into every decision. Wealth without wellbeing is a liability, but together, they create unstoppable momentum." Sheena Walker

As I went to the pool, my dad encouraged me: "Be the best you can be at your training this morning, Sheena." Little did I know that my 5 a.m. swimming club would leave such a lasting impression during those early hours between 5 a.m. and 7 a.m., instilling a routine that nurtured determination and performance for life. Looking back, it is intriguing how energised and happy I felt, experiencing a daily sense of reaching for the stars.

As I matured, this routine became the cornerstone of my high-performance journey. Imagine adopting my 5 a.m. pool routine; it could change your life forever. Visualise being a business executive with a winning strategy to enhance productivity in every aspect of your daily life.

Successful business people and world-class athletes schedule daily "Quality Recovery" time to recharge and refresh their bodies, preparing them for the next session. They do not train non-stop; they recognise the importance of well-being. Figures such as Jeff Bezos, Tony Robbins, Andy Murray, Ronaldo, and Messi incorporate "Quality Recovery" programmes into their daily routines, focusing on mental, physical, and overall well-being.

The onset of the COVID-19 pandemic in March 2020 changed the lives of business professionals. We witnessed redundancies, business closures, staff layoffs, and people retraining for new careers. I've observed that people are working increasingly long hours to maintain their jobs. Some teams require more effective recruitment and selection procedures. Recruiting the right person at the right time and place should be paramount, not left to chance.

Have you noticed the myths and untruths on social media and in the news? Sensationalism strikes every public-sector organisation, resulting in absenteeism, staff feeling undervalued, and a high level of mental health issues.

Senior executives proudly declare, "I work 80 hours or more every week." However, in the modern age, they often lack a personal life. Questioning the persuasive presence of media, including TV, newspapers, and phones, as well as excessive working hours, is essential.

The content and experiences from these outlets can consume our minds, profoundly affecting our emotional state and influencing how we behave, interact, think, and converse. As an executive, you may feel your life is oversaturated with media buzz. Taking a break to free up thinking space, rather than being constantly bombarded with external signals, could be highly beneficial.

So, how can you create a pool of new well-being opportunities? It is time to invest in the mindset, determination, and mental preparedness of a top athlete, or someone like Tony Robbins, who actively advocates for well-being. I've personally participated in his mental mastery and self-improvement programmes.

This chapter will address the question: "What is the best advice I can offer the team?" Teaching them the principles, processes, and systems of health mastery can lead to fewer mistakes and provide peace and serenity during quality recovery time. Self-improvement and well-being are essential for being exceptional. After all, how can one work effectively with others without first mastering these themselves?

Visualise winning ways with Walker's 5 a.m. Club Routine. Learn to centre yourself, enjoy quiet time, reconnect with your mind, and embrace creative thinking in your performance. This journey involves reflecting on how you present yourself and discovering skills you may not even have been aware of. You might initially feel something is missing during fasting, but that emptiness creates space for an expansive, clutter-free life. How would you rate your physical and psychological well-being, workload, and quality recovery time on a scale of zero to ten? Does it truly exist, yes or no?

Director Note: *Let's revise your productivity formula now. Embrace difference with the Walker-Winning Ways of Health. Is it time to establish a new routine?*

Your A1 Lane: Crafting a New Routine

Imagine discovering your unique blend of wellness. What might that look like? It could involve 6 a.m. yoga or the gym, but it could also be entirely different. It's about having practical tools to help you reclaim the power around you when you need it most. This journey isn't about believing you're the most beautiful person in the world, but rather about knowing you deserve to live your best life as a top player.

Focus on well-being intentions in your business, career, and daily life. Imagine the freedom you'll experience when you're no longer fixated on working endlessly every day. Visualise more adventures, downtime, laughter, and moments of triumph, bringing you a more vibrant day. It's time to release chaotic daily habits and create more space for creative thinking. Are you in?

What if I could show you where to discover the initial steps on that frictionless path to claiming your Yellow Brick Road of success? Let's conquer negativity and equip you with the tools to embrace your authentic self. Imagine cultivating healthy thoughts and habits that truly endure.

Treat yourself with kindness by exploring new ways to cultivate healthier mindsets and habits. You might feel like skipping the gym when it seems overwhelming, but have you considered roller skating, swimming, or walking? They're all excellent for your well-being.

Your new intentions may take you beyond the Yellow Brick Road. What needs to happen between now and 31 December 2026? What will this year cost you, just another year? What single habit could you adopt to elevate all your other habits, enhancing your creativity, productivity, prosperity, and impact?

I teach business professionals to break performance boundaries. Many spend little to no time maintaining their well-being. So, what about breaking free and changing your intentions for well-being?

Are you establishing new routines to enhance performance? When setting goals, define success with your internal scorecard and refrain from measuring it by others' definitions of success.

Find your own quality standards rather than those the world imposes on you. It is a principle worth holding on to. Surround yourself with mentors and begin to feel fabulous.

In the corporate world, I became an expert in scorecards, an effective way to measure critical business success factors. Each week, we tracked deliverable outcomes across all facets of the business, including marketing, sales, operations, finance, and, crucially, staffing, retention, recruitment, and absenteeism. Now picture a visual representation of your daily life using a scorecard you can assess and learn from.

Why do so many of us doubt ourselves, looking in the mirror and comparing ourselves to our colleagues, peers, and others in the same industry, wishing we resembled them? What is it about the world we inhabit? When we desire to change how we look, feel, and think, it's often tempting to remain inactive. Let us first explore these notions. Did you know that, aerodynamically, bumblebees shouldn't be able to fly? Yet nobody told them they couldn't, so they did. Where will you fly to?

You must become an A1 player in vitality to lead your industry. You can only produce masterful work if you are healthy and capable of managing a substantial workload. Would you agree? You are talented, knowledgeable, and experienced; you are enough. It is not about appearance, but rather internal mental preparedness, which becomes second nature to an athlete. You don't have to wake up every day loving every inch of yourself; however, it does mean shifting your focus from your current state of self-assessment towards setting new intentions and considering how you feel inside.

Director Note: *Time to Visualise, An A1 Routine of Champions.*

That energy, grit, mental preparedness, and a fresh approach to focusing your intentions will enable you to thrive in both business and life. When you begin to feel negative, it's essential to acknowledge and transform those feelings. You must take ownership of your life and elevate yourself to new heights. When you feel good, your appearance will naturally improve. Imagine how wonderful it would be if you could create and define your own standard as a premier player of vitality. It's time to say, "I can."

The Five Intentions for A1 Vitality in a Perfect Morning

Why Establish That New A1 Lane?

What is the one thing you can do to significantly improve your life? Begin your day with a morning routine. A morning routine instils intention into your day, offering structure, design, and purpose. Picture yourself navigating each step calmly and composedly. You know precisely what is required of you and when. Are you with me?

There are no surprises to keep you scrambling; you will remember what truly matters. Understanding the essence of this provides clarity, meaning, and direction. Although clarity is a simple word, it is a crucial component of motivation and inspiration. It enables you to understand who you are, where you're going, and how you will get there. Five, four, three, two, one, here we go!

Let's reflect on my 5 a.m. routine. The Peak Performance Pyramid consists of mindset, performance, and personal best. What would that entail for you? Developing your movement, mindset, and memory routine begins with five minutes each, contributing to the 10-10-10 formula. For me, it was strengthening my swimming habit.

Now is the moment to seek new experiences and embrace life's limitless possibilities. If you feel unsure where to start, don't fret, it's time to leap into the champion's lane.

Let's play to win the best game of your life. It all begins with a fresh morning routine, establishing new patterns and habits.

Lane 1 for Champions: That's You

Begin your day with energy, determination, and a focused mindset to excel in both your professional and personal life. Recognise negativity and transform it into positivity as you take charge of your journey.

Picture yourself reaching new heights, radiating confidence and vitality. Crafting excellence as an A1 player means focusing on three essentials:

One: Movement My exercise of choice is swimming in the local pool.

Two: Mindfulness Relaxation audio and positive affirmations.

Three: Memory A blend of podcasts, videos, and a chapter from a book.

Director Note: *Choose the 3M from your Peak Performance Pyramid.*

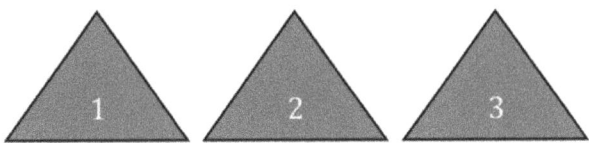

Routine triggers new brain patterns

Starting a new routine is challenging because it requires effort to establish it as a habit. It's easy to slip back into old patterns, particularly when feeling tired or disheartened.

This is why your first step involves understanding your purpose. Know why you're striving for a better morning, and say these words aloud every day when you first get up to remind yourself of them. Are you seeking greater productivity, a calmer day, or enhanced confidence? You need to decide this before you begin.

Lane 2: Baby Steps

You can adjust your focus, energy, productivity, or sleep schedule, or even make significant changes to your mornings, if you tend to burn out quickly. This is why it's crucial to devise a plan in advance, so you know what changes will take effect and when. For instance, if you usually wake up at 9:00 a.m. but want to rise at 7:00 a.m., you'll need to introduce gradual adjustments. In the first week, you might wake at 8:45, the following week at 8:30, and so on.

Lane 3: Commit to Consistency

You will succeed in building new habits only if you consistently engage in the same actions. Recognise that you cannot approach this with half measures. Commit to following the routine every day. A swimmer doesn't stop halfway down the lane!

Lane 4: Craft an Evening Routine

Your mornings will improve if you complement them with a thoughtful evening routine, such as setting a regular bedtime. Evenings are also a great time to prepare for the next day by laying out your clothes or organising what you'll need.

Lane 5: Create Your Performance Routine

The key to establishing a routine is addressing all areas of your well-being. For example, exercise and a balanced diet support physical health; meditation and prayer nurture spiritual well-being; learning and positive self-talk strengthen your mental state; while journaling and affirmations enhance emotional health. The aim is to achieve a harmonious balance each day. Personal discipline is like a muscle, the more you stretch it, the stronger it becomes.

Follow these steps closely for lasting results. Take heart, there's a routine to do all these things, and you only need five steps to make your day flow smoothly. Increasing self-control in one area of your life can elevate it in all others, as one life-changing habit has the power to influence everything else you do.

Understand what it's all about and bring clarity to your day. Clarity may be a simple word, but it's essential for motivation and inspiration. Knowing who you are, where you're going, and how you'll get there will help you create the ideal morning routine. Now, you're ready to start your day.

Director Note: *New Habit Redesign Your Emotional State through Resilience Re-engineering*

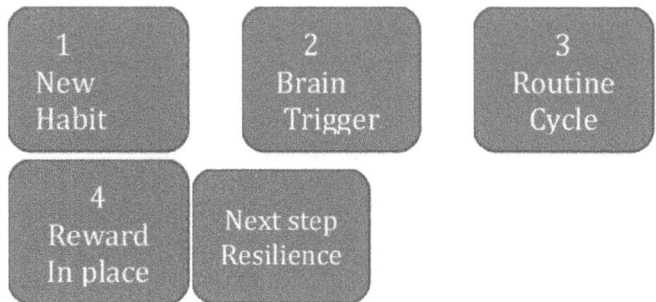

Great CEOs and professionals who recognise the importance of being fitter, healthier, and more successful also possess a strong emotional state. They remain cool, calm, and collected, fostering balance and resilience. Their conversations are impactful, powerful, and persuasive, helping to break bad habits and establish healthier ones.

The principles of developing mind–body connections are at the forefront for professionals who understand the relationship between body and mind, as well as the significance of mental preparedness in business. Taking positive action to feel energised grants tremendous power and impact, enabling you to expand your influence and success many times over. Can you visualise achieving excellence in all areas in pursuit of victory?

I recall attending a personal development event a few years ago where Tony Robbins was the main speaker. As he entered the arena, he looked slightly flustered but quickly displayed his trademark energy, passion, and charisma. I smiled when he mentioned spending thirty minutes on his trampoline before going on stage. Why? Because it was a genuine example of conditioning the brain through anaerobic exercise before performing.

Do you see what I'm getting at? Just as elite athletes know the necessity of training both body and mind for success, business professionals must also embrace mental preparedness alongside a healthy, balanced physique if they wish to stand out.

Research has recently exposed numerous myths surrounding resilience, recovery, well-being, and mindfulness. Imagine living in the present moment, cultivating calm, balance, and a fresh perspective at work, in your shed, or during your downtime. This programme is designed to help you grow into a new version of yourself.

Director Note: *Consider the Self-Mastery Question: Am I an Economy, First Class, or A1 Player?*

Do or Ditch Brain Clutter

World-class professionals take media breaks, using them as opportunities to declutter their minds. Recharging and maintaining balance are essential for creativity and innovation. Many organisations are now establishing well-being programmes and safeguarding protected time for staff. When employees feel valued through such measures, sickness and absenteeism drop, morale improves, and performance benefits across the board.

So why do many organisations wait until absenteeism is high and staff feel undervalued before taking action on recovery and protected time? Is your organisation guilty of treating it as an afterthought?

Quality Recovery Builds Resilience Creating White Space

We've already discussed managing your mornings as a fundamental skill for becoming an exceptional A1 player, using the start of your day to drive success. One common myth, however, is that the morning routine itself is the only time for profound peace and recovery. Why is tranquillity now regarded as the new luxury, highlighting the significance of quality recovery time? Athletes never overlook the importance of refreshing, recharging, and protecting their physical health, it would be unthinkable.

Travelling across the globe, I've been struck by how often people work close to 20 hours a day, believing it builds resilience. Yet when breaks and holidays are neglected, burnout becomes inevitable. Staff shortages compound this problem. So, how do we shift from burnout to balance?

What if you treated your brain like a muscle in the gym, giving it aerobic workouts and conditioning? Brain training is vital. In many ways, recovery reflects the importance of being a great transformation student, and it is a complete game-changer.

I'll share how to centre yourself, embrace quiet time, and reconnect with your mind through fasting. I'll also introduce the concept of *white space*, encouraging reflection on performance and presentation, and helping you uncover skills you may not know you possess. Although fasting may initially feel like something is missing, that emptiness creates space for clarity and a clutter-free life.

Sheena's Mind, Brain Speaker Shed

On shift one day, I spoke with Douglas, my First Responder buddy, about the speaker shed at the bottom of my garden. We laughed as I explained how it was my white space for brainpower thinking, but how cold it was without heating. Seconds later, Douglas, an electrician and health and safety expert, said, *"That's not a problem. What if I put electricity in your shed?"* He did, and it works brilliantly. You, too, can create your own white space, with or without a special Douglas.

Now I spend time daily in my back-garden shed, regardless of the weather. It is my space for quality recovery, reflection, and creativity. Away from my desk, I can review my work, rethink challenges, and reset direction. After an hour, I return refreshed with new ideas and clarity. Here's a self-mastery question: *What should I do, or let go of?* Cultivating white space gives you the tranquillity to answer it.

Busting the Myths of Resilience

There are countless misconceptions about mindset, resilience, and recovery. Too often, fitness gurus and business leaders promote workloads that push people beyond their limits, claiming it builds resilience. I've spoken with countless professionals stuck in endless cycles of overwork, emails from dawn until night, like hamsters on a wheel. Many are simply exhausted.

So why does the military-style mindset of pushing through persist? Athletes, whether a boxer going one more round, a footballer playing an extra hour, or a rugby player driving through fatigue, are often told that endurance equals resilience. But science tells us otherwise.

When I researched this a few years ago, I had to change my own perspective. In fact, lack of recovery undermines resilience and prosperity. Studies reveal a direct correlation between insufficient recovery and workplace safety issues. Many major incidents, including building accidents and fires, have been linked to long hours and a lack of quality checks. Is it any wonder?

Director Note: *Your Work is Your Craft; Your Life is an Art.*

Resilience: How You Recharge, Not How You Persevere

Harvard researchers Michelle Gielan and Shawn Achor have shown that resilience and well-being are not fuelled by endless work, but by ensuring daily quality recovery time.

Yet many people finish at the office only to open their laptops the moment they get home. A study in Norway found that 8% of the population are workaholics, workaholism is now a major health and fitness issue.

True resilience can be understood simply: strive, pave, recover, then try again. Both brain and body must continually restore balance after exertion. Spending too much time in the performance zone creates imbalance, unless it's matched by recovery in equal measure. The harder you push, the more you must prioritise restorative practices.

The key is to understand that rest and recovery are not the same. Stopping work is not the same as recovering. To build resilience as an athlete, musician, or business leader, internal recovery must include relaxation, mindfulness, and mental preparation. Without this ongoing effort, burnout is inevitable.

Consider whether a high-performance coach has to persuade Andy Murray, Messi, or Ronaldo to take time out. No! They would think that was bloody stupid. They understand that recovery is a habit that fosters both internal and external well-being, ultimately promoting overall physical and mental wellness. What about you?

Now is the time to cultivate resilience through a robust recovery strategy and access the essential resources needed to establish both internal and external recovery periods. The process is simple: set aside quality recovery time to walk or visit a park during the day, breaking up your work routine. One effective method is to work for fifty minutes, then take a ten-minute break. Also, protect time in your calendar for calls, digital technology is one of the biggest drains on resilience.

Director Note: *Resilience is How You Recharge, Not How You Endure.*

Embrace a New Wellness Routine: Sleep or Swim

Have you ever heard someone say, *"I don't require much sleep, I only got three hours last night, and I feel great"*? Sleep scientists argue that sleep is more crucial for our health than diet or exercise. I find the research on how sleep influences performance fascinating. I'm not a good sleeper myself, and only recently have I been working with professionals in the well-being and fitness sector to develop better habits.

Is Elon Musk Working in Economy or First Class?

Elon Musk, CEO of Tesla, has long disregarded the science showing that sleep deprivation and burnout undermine performance. Yet, when he took the stand last month, he admitted: *"I had trouble sleeping last night, so I'm not at my best."* A change of heart, perhaps? Was this the result of months of reduced brain function? Is sleep essential to our identity, shaping how we move, speak, work, and perform? Or does it come down to poor habits? I'll let you decide.

Can you recall the last time you felt refreshed and brand new? Can you wake up without an alarm? Or do you wake with your first thought being, *"I need a cup of coffee"*? If you keep a diary, you should aim for seven to nine hours' sleep each night. My Fitbit tracks this daily. A family member of mine starts work between 5.00 and 6.00 a.m., and I can't reach him after 9.00 p.m., he's already preparing for the next day. He has his sleep routine down to a fine art. And if I need an early airport run, I know I can rely on his alarm call.

Arianna Huffington supports the resilient recharge theory, which states that overwork and exhaustion are the enemies of resilience. Habits learned in youth can carry over and magnify in the working world. In *The Sleep Revolution*, she argues that people sacrifice sleep for productivity at their peril. She emphasises living in the present moment to foster calm, balance, and perspective, at work, in the shed, or on days off, while calling for a revolution in how we approach sleep.

There is clear evidence that fewer than six hours of sleep weakens your mood and is a major lifestyle risk factor. Even one week of poor sleep can disrupt blood sugar levels, putting you at risk of becoming pre-diabetic.

In short, sleep deprivation and poor sleep patterns increase the likelihood of blocked or brittle arteries, setting you on the path to cardiovascular disease. Will this make you change your habits? It certainly would me.

Director Note: *Rest and Recovery Are Different. Be in the Lane of Wellness.*

Does Streamlining Sleep Create Physical and Psychological Preparedness?

Matthew Walker, professor at the University of California, Berkeley, argues that inadequate sleep is harmful. His studies show that the less you sleep, the shorter your lifespan, making quality sleep an essential daily habit. His research presents a holistic view of well-being, linking poor sleep to both physical disease and mental disorders.

Reflecting on my student days, I now realise how much sleep deprivation held me back. The brain performs diverse functions, learning, memory, logical decision-making, that are all impaired by poor sleep. Staying up late to study is not only unwise but counterproductive.

We can agree that physical and mental preparedness begins with a good night's sleep. Athletes certainly believe so, heading to bed at a sensible hour because they know that without rest, their results would be very different.

You may recall athletes being dropped during the World Cup and Euros, commentators acted surprised. Yet sometimes players risk going out late the night before a crucial match. A manager drops them because he doesn't want to risk poor performance. If sleep is critical to physical and emotional well-being, why do leaders and influential people still boast about getting by on so little? The pressures of our economy have undoubtedly disrupted natural sleep cycles.

Director Note: *Streamline Your Sleep or Sink into Low Performance.*

Well-being and Women in Power, or Not?

Say Yes

A University of Southampton study found that women were more vulnerable to sleep deprivation during lockdown. Factors included disrupted routines, no commute, working from home, negative news cycles, closed gyms, cancelled social outings. All of this shifted natural sleep patterns. Sleep deprivation led to difficulty thinking, increased worry, and changes in behaviour. Have we become a nation of the "lazy brigade," addicted to mobile phones 24/7?

Mobile Phone: Do You Use It 24/7?

In today's fast-paced digital age, smartphones are indispensable, our gateway to information, communication, and entertainment. Yet constant use has given rise to smartphone addiction. Understanding why people are so deeply attached to their phones is vital, as is recognising the need for digital detox.

Do you keep your phone on 24/7? Answering calls during meetings signals that the caller is more important than the people in front of you. I've stopped using devices in the early evening to improve my sleep routine. Arianna Huffington and others have even suggested that phones in the bedroom can emit radiation.

A friend once told me he goes to bed with his laptop. An unbelievably poor habit! Why would you want your phone in the bedroom? This is addictive behaviour. Limiting mobile use for at least two hours before bed can dramatically improve sleep quality. More importantly, the device is simply *not there*. That is what A1 players do?

Director Note: *Time to Detox from Mobile Phone Addiction.*

Sheena L.C. Walker

Low Energy, Low Performance

Have you ever woken up and thought, *I can't face the day*? How you wake will determine your energy levels and performance, and sleep is, without a doubt, part of that feel-good factor. Feeling healthy, confident, and happy can be summarised in two words: recharged and energised. If that's what you want, then focus on getting a good night's sleep.

Do you do this now? I sometimes browse social media before bed and send messages to my family, but keeping my mind engaged with technology can make it harder to fall asleep. Recently, I've been watching Sky and Netflix and enjoying some excellent recommended series. However, I noticed my sleep quality deteriorated after watching Netflix. Why? Because it made it difficult for me to relax and drift off.

As we spend more time with technology, we need time to unwind and prepare for the night. Recovery. Adequate sleep is essential for a healthy lifestyle, offering unique benefits for heart health, digestion, memory, innovation, and creativity. The more I hear people speak about insomnia, the more I realise that we must master the skill of well-being and become extraordinary producers. Bedtime must be treated as a priority.

What if you scheduled an appointment in your diary for your nightly routine? Prepare for a brilliant night's sleep. Jack Black, who wrote *Mind Store*, suggests keeping a notebook by your bed to jot down thoughts if you wake up with them. He also recommends affirmations before sleep. Consider incorporating more self-care and self-love through these affirmations.

Director Note: *Be Ready to Change to Zone of Genius Thinking*

Is There a New Approach to Lane 4 Breathing?

Breathe in inspiration; breathe out wisdom. One key characteristic of a professional speaker is a high emotional state. What do I mean by that? It's in how you walk, talk, and present yourself. Why do some people appear cool, calm, and collected, while others seem frantic?

During my speaking sessions, we practise breathing exercises that incorporate presence and posture. The effects of breathing techniques on body and mind can send a very different signal to your audience. That's why I was fascinated when I read about Wim Hof's methods for well-being and maximising human potential beyond what we may believe possible.

Dancing on Ice: The Cold-Water Theory

The "Iceman" theory has brought powerful health practices into mainstream well-being, harnessing the power of water, breath control, and cold-water training. Would you stop and listen?

Wim Hof's beliefs about human potential have been the subject of extensive scientific research. He argues we can achieve anything we set our minds to, and that human potential is limitless within 39 days of practice, creating radiance and even extending lifespan. He believes extreme cold exposure can heal both body and mind. I would always recommend, however, that you discuss this with your GP.

His research suggests that water exposure should become part of our daily routine. Tony Robbins also subjects himself daily to breath work and cold-water immersion. Studies have shown significant improvements in energy, well-being, immune system strength, and the management of inflammation and cardiovascular health.

As a keen swimmer used to cold water, I know the energy I feel leaping out of a pool is nothing compared to plunging 100 feet beneath a frozen lake. A study published by Redbones University in the Netherlands, led by Dr Cox and Dr Picus, examined responses to Hof's methods. Remember the Ice Bucket Challenge we all saw on social media? People tipped buckets of freezing water over themselves, many found it uncomfortable, and yet Hof's methods are rooted in the same principle: using cold to rewire our resilience.

One of the benefits of Wim's approach is its impact on athletes. He works with world-class performers who want to push further without relying on drugs or artificial enhancement. The method provides a genuine competitive edge. What if you could increase your well-being the same way?

The Iceman's method is simple and effective, combining three pillars: breathing exercises, cold-water training, and mental commitment. Who would have thought deep breathing alone could boost performance? With the right mindset, cold-water immersion and breathwork can elevate your game beyond expectations.

Your life will never be the same once you activate this streamlined approach to well-being. Hof's methods can prevent burnout, reduce stress, accelerate recovery, and improve sleep, supporting A1 athletes and business professionals alike with creativity, focus, and mental clarity. Part of my own new routine includes incorporating his methods for peak well-being.

My Corporate Athlete wellness programme will change your life. Increasing focus, energy, and effectiveness by 30% daily is not complicated. My clients master three key areas to foster renewal, recharge their minds, and redesign their approach, ultimately creating extraordinary mental preparedness in the world of work.

Director Note: *To Have a Fantastic Business, Develop a Fabulous Well-Being Lifestyle*

Sixteen Ways to Feel Amazing as an A1 Performer

- Put a curfew on all tech. No devices in the bedroom.

- Be more physically active during the day and take breaks.

- Use three new movements to build fresh brain patterns.

- Practise breathing techniques to enhance emotional presence.

- Set a curfew on your eating habits.

- Give your digestive system rest at night.

- No coffee after noon, support better sleep.

- Block non-negotiable time for significant projects.

- Schedule uninterrupted priority time tomorrow.

- Say: *I can change today into the best version of tomorrow.*

- Say: *I will demonstrate acts of kindness tomorrow.*

- Begin self-care and self-love with design thinking and health.

- Create new intentions to drive better decisions.

- Carve out routines to boost performance.

- Surround yourself with those who celebrate you, not just tolerate you.

- Commit to bold intentions and ambitious career goals.

Say Yes

Director Note

Chapter 8: Well-Being for Winners

- A high performer protects their energy like a precious asset. Well-being is not a pause it's a power strategy.

- Start your day with one elite-level habit.

- Reframe rest as recovery, not retreat.

- Remove one energy drain from your daily landscape.

- Choose one practice that upgrades mind-body-business synergy.

Sheena

Say Yes to Becoming the CEO of Your Life

Different Stages Bonus Training

1. **The Power of Vocal Dynamics Podcast**
   https://shorturl.at/mQJB7

2. **Five Secrets of Securing That New Career**
   https://shorturl.at/wqs6S

3. **24 Celebrity Speaking Tips**
   https://bit.ly/3Wwnb5W

4. **The Art of Speaking Framework**
   https://bit.ly/3SGMXm8

5. **Video: Choosing a Coach**
   https://youtu.be/HKQ-paX1aiU

6. **Customer Experience**
   https://bit.ly/3CJk5Uz

7. **Wellbeing Wim Hof**
   https://www.wimhofmethod.com

8. **About Sheena: Get in Touch Today**
   https://card.pramaze.com/sheena-walker

9. **Six-Week Masterclass**
   https://shorturl.at/SSFP7

10. **Please Get in Touch to Arrange a Shaping Design**
    www.sheenawalker.com

    https://www.sheenawalker.com/book

11. Book Me to Speak at Your Organisation

https://shorturl.at/PJ4Yy

The Luxury Coach for CEOs: Expert in Performance-Based Speaking and Business Branding

Are you ready to elevate your speaking skills, master your business branding, and deliver impeccable pitches that captivate and convert? You've come to the right place if you wish to lead, be unmatched, and confidently command the stage.

As a results-driven performance coach, I specialise in high-performance speaking, business branding, and presentation mastery. Whether you need to refine your keynote delivery, craft a compelling business pitch, or build a magnetic personal brand, I offer elite coaching tailored for ambitious professionals, CEOs, and executives who demand world-class results.

Performance Services

- **Presenting Essentials:** Learn to speak with impact, engage your audience, and command the room. Whether you're just starting out or refining your presence, I will help you deliver with clarity, confidence, and charisma.

- **Business Branding:** Your Brand Is Your Power. I assist CEOs, entrepreneurs, and thought leaders in creating a powerful, luxury personal brand that establishes them as trailblazers in their industry.

- **Perfect Pitches:** If you're pitching for investment, sales, or leadership buy-in, you need more than just a script; you require a strategy. I will help you create a pitch that is persuasive, memorable, and designed for success.

- **Keynote & Public Speaking Mastery:** Whether you're delivering a TED-style talk, a corporate keynote, or an industry presentation, I will showcase how to command the stage, engage with your audience, and create a lasting impact.

- **1:1 Elite Coaching:** Partner with me for customised, high-performance coaching tailored to meet your goals. From honing your vocal dynamics to mastering executive presence, I offer the techniques and strategies that enable you to stand out.

What Sets Me Apart?

- **World-Class Expertise:** With a solid track record in coaching CEOs, executives, and top professionals, I understand what it takes to attain podium-level success.

- **Performance-Based Approach:** I incorporate presentation skills, business psychology, and high-performance strategies to ensure you're not merely speaking. You're influencing, persuading, and leading.

- **Proven Results:** My clients have successfully secured winning pitches, obtained significant deals, enhanced their executive presence, and established brands that command premium positioning.

- **Luxury, High-End Coaching Experience:** As the Luxury Coach for CEOs, I offer a high-calibre, results-oriented experience tailored for professionals who aim to excel in a competitive world.

Who Is This For?

- CEOs and executives seeking to enhance their leadership presence

- Entrepreneurs and business owners requiring a powerful brand and pitch

- Speakers and presenters aiming to deliver with impact and authority

- Thought leaders striving to become the go-to expert in their industry

- Professionals preparing for career-defining presentations and pitches

Ready to Take the Stage Like a Professional?

Let's transform your speaking, branding, and pitching skills into a significant advantage. Schedule a session with me today and begin positioning yourself as a world-class leader.

First, Be The Best, Then Be First

Sheena

Opportunity to Work With Sheena

1. The Art and Craft of Stagecraft

Your presence is priceless and more important than ever in your career.

You may not be a public speaker, but you still have a right to be heard.

My on-demand online course will help you present your voice in a polished, powerful way and, most importantly, develop your style, as it always should be.

The Art of Speaking to Conquer Nerves is the essential foundation to step up in your business, working at your own pace.

https://shorturl.at/SyeUx
www.sheenawalker.com

2. Invest in Our Luxury Flagship Program

Welcome to the **90-Day Executive Ascendancy**, a bespoke, performance-driven pathway for ambitious executives, thought leaders, and entrepreneurs ready to dominate their commercial space.

This is not just a coaching program. It is an elite-level recalibration of your personal brand, positioning, and performance.

In just 90 days, you will gain the strategic precision of a world-class brand, the presence of a commanding speaker, and the clarity to convert attention into authority and profit.

Your message will land. Your leadership will scale. Your commercial influence will rise.

Every step is designed for transformation, crafted for professionals who are done playing small and are ready to lead with distinction.

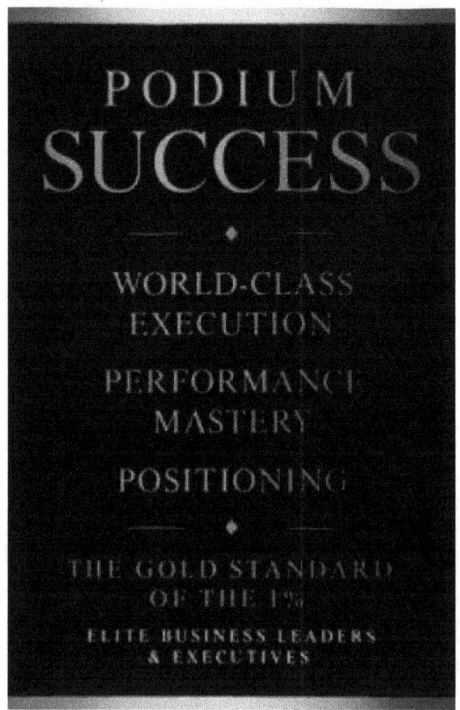

3. The Power of Vocal Dynamics Business School

Welcome to **The Power of Vocal Dynamics**, where each episode is crafted to help you unlock the secrets of elite-level communication.

With over 300 actionable mini masterclasses, this podcast is your go-to resource for mastering business skills and performance speaking techniques that put you in the top 1%.

Designed for ambitious professionals, each episode equips you with insights and strategies to sharpen your influence, command attention, and achieve extraordinary results.

Thus, you can take your presence to the next level in any setting.

https://the-different-stages-celebrity-speaker.onpodium.com/

Book a Shaping Call:

https://card.pramaze.com/sheena-walker

The Art and Craft of Stagecraft